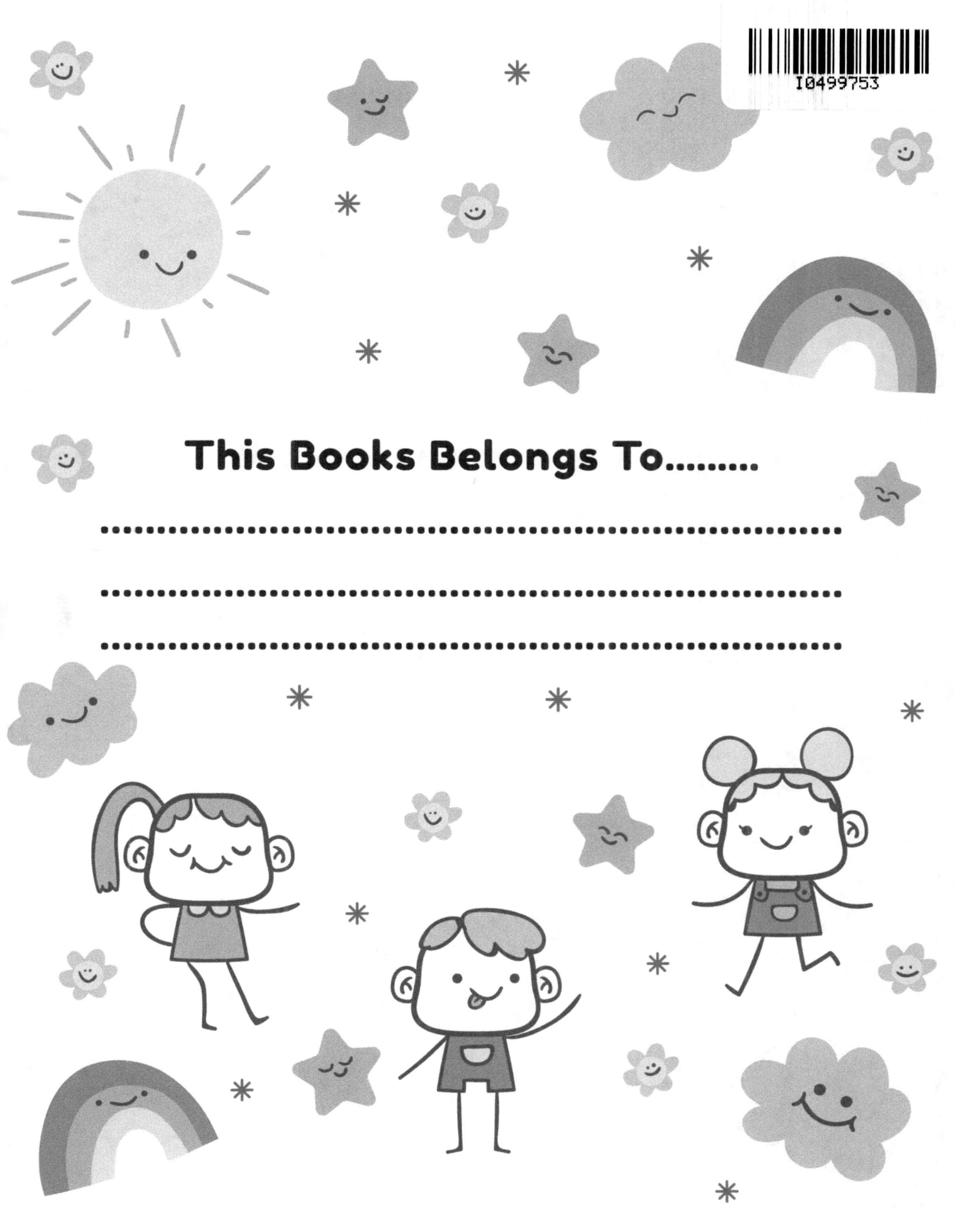

This Books Belongs To.........

....

....

....

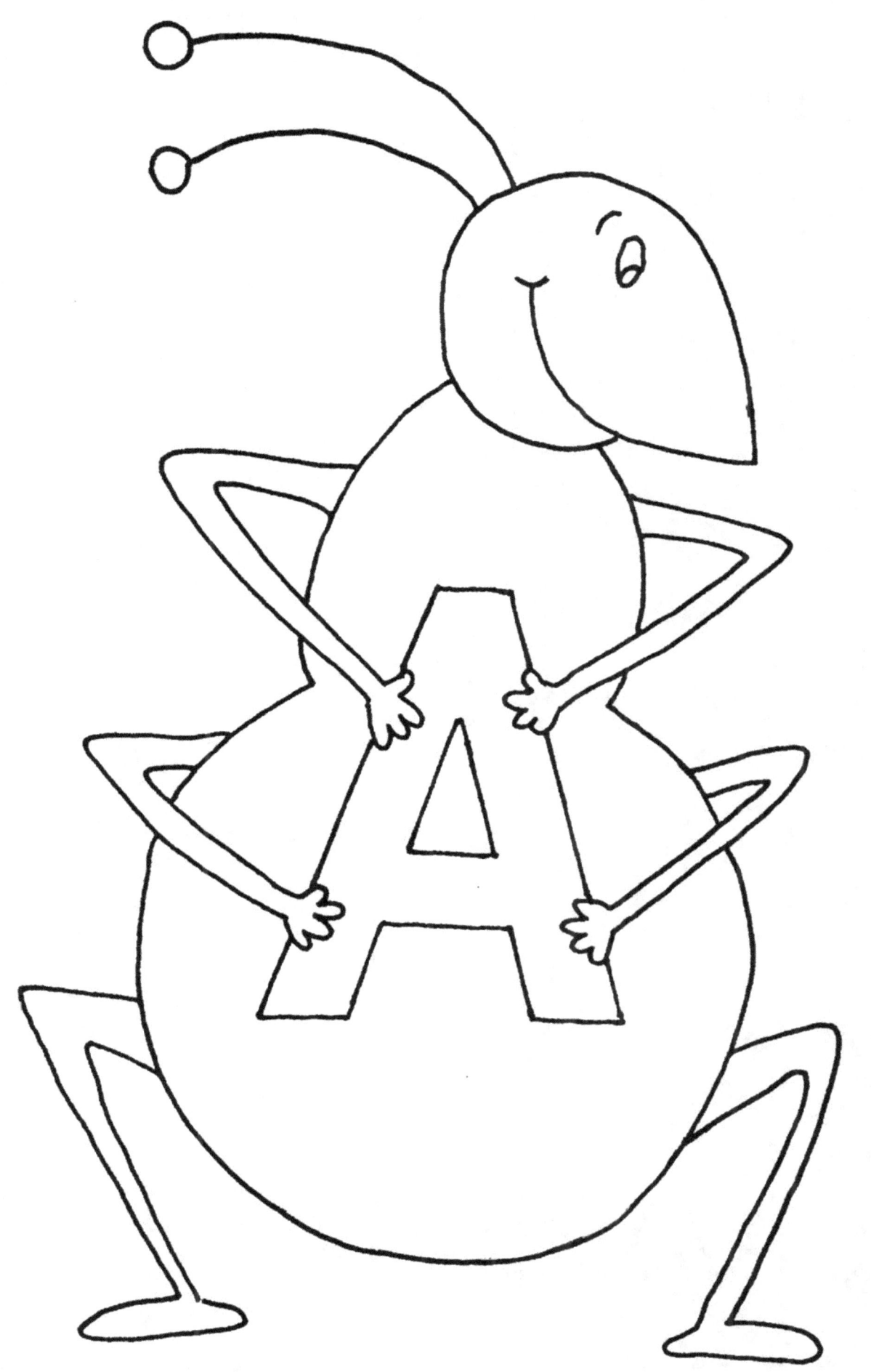

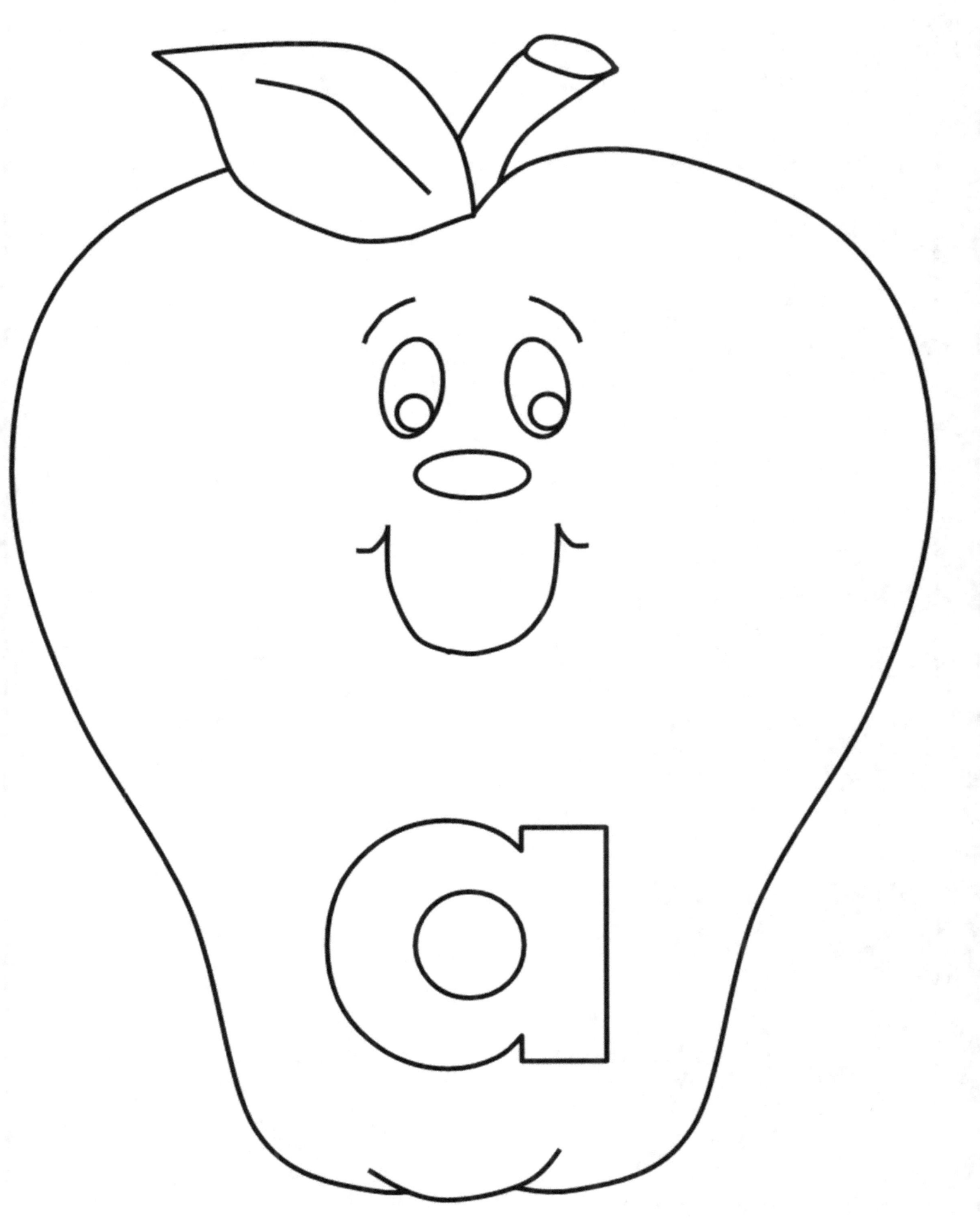

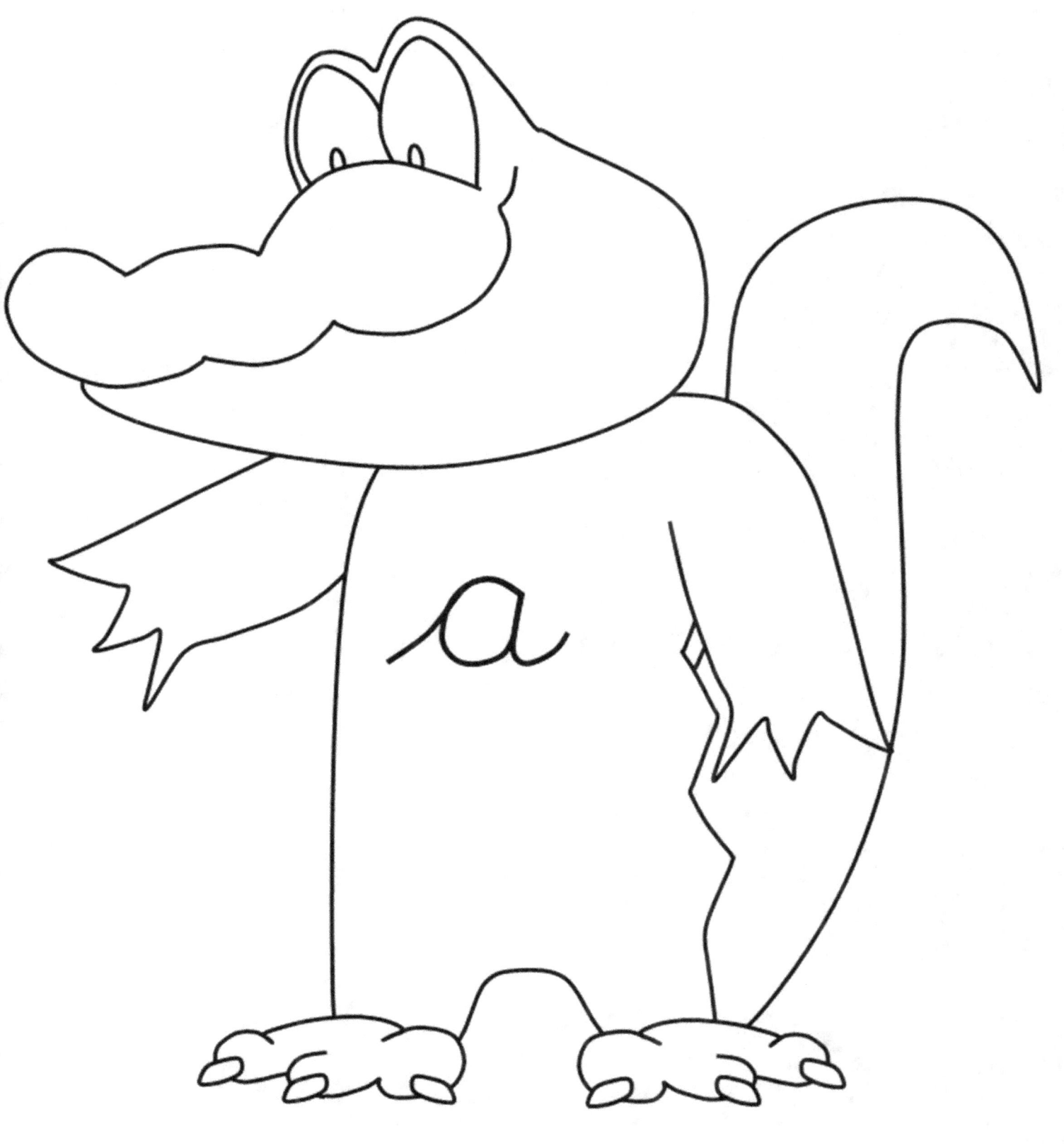

Trace the steps for making the letter a on the following line.

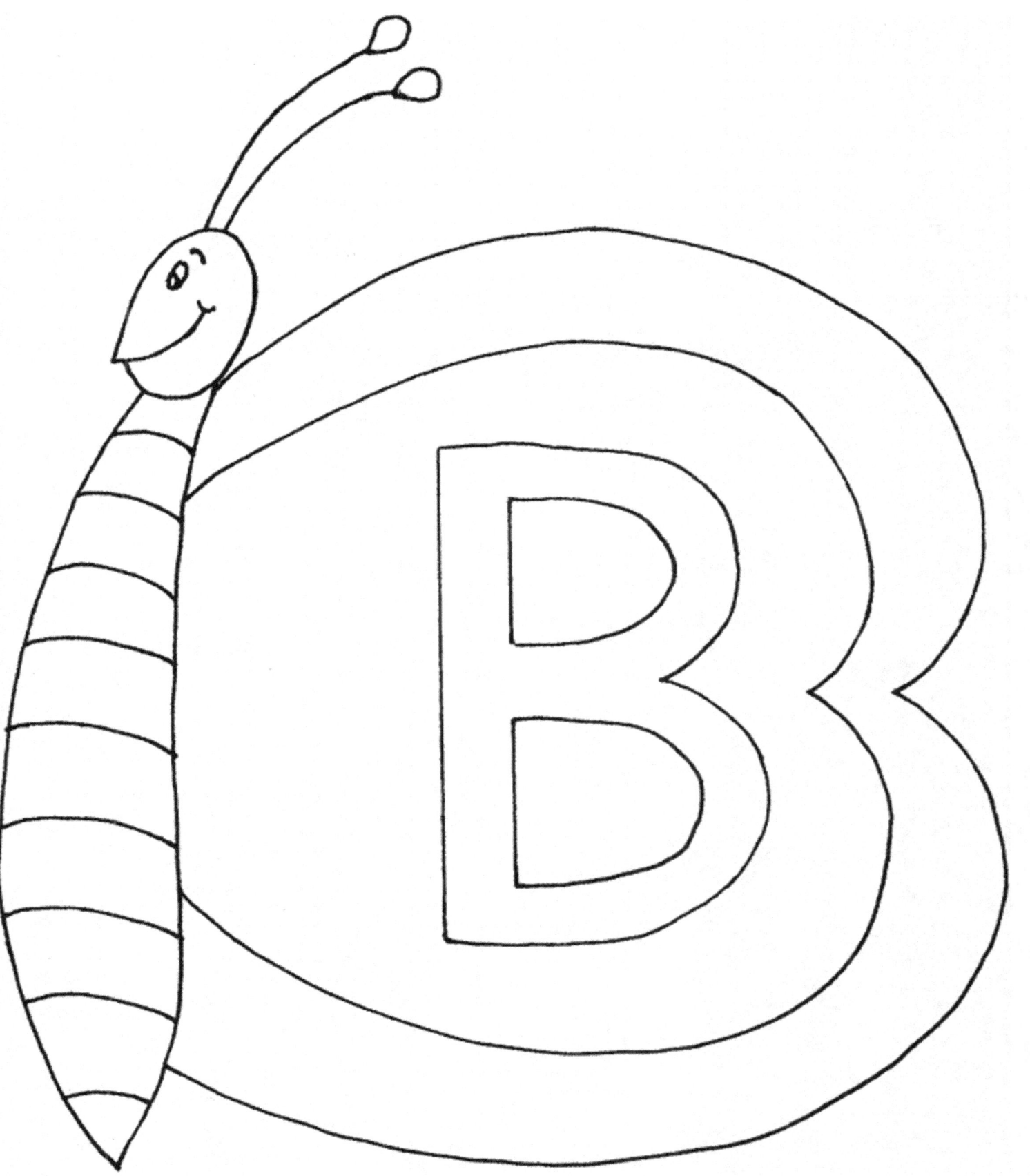

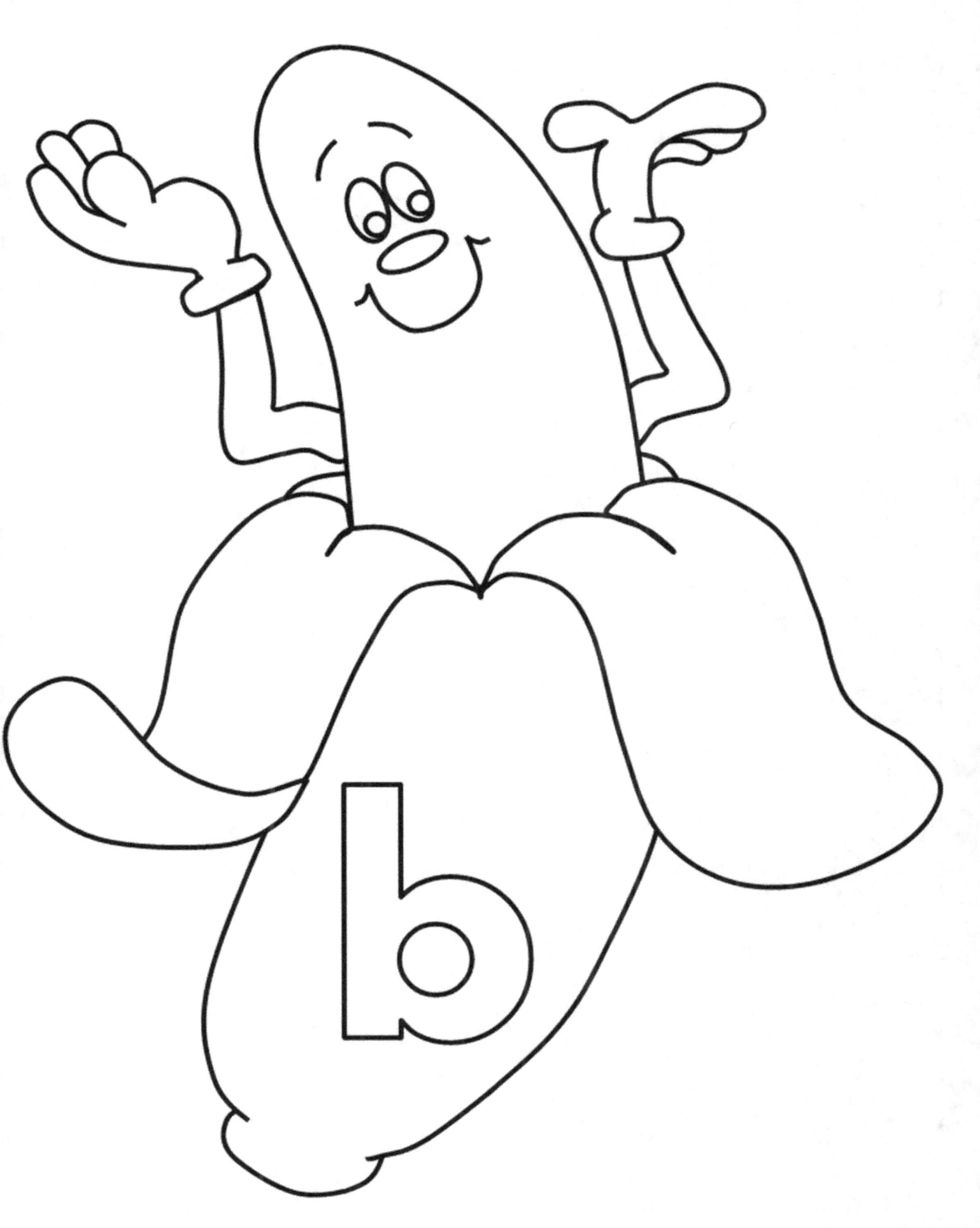

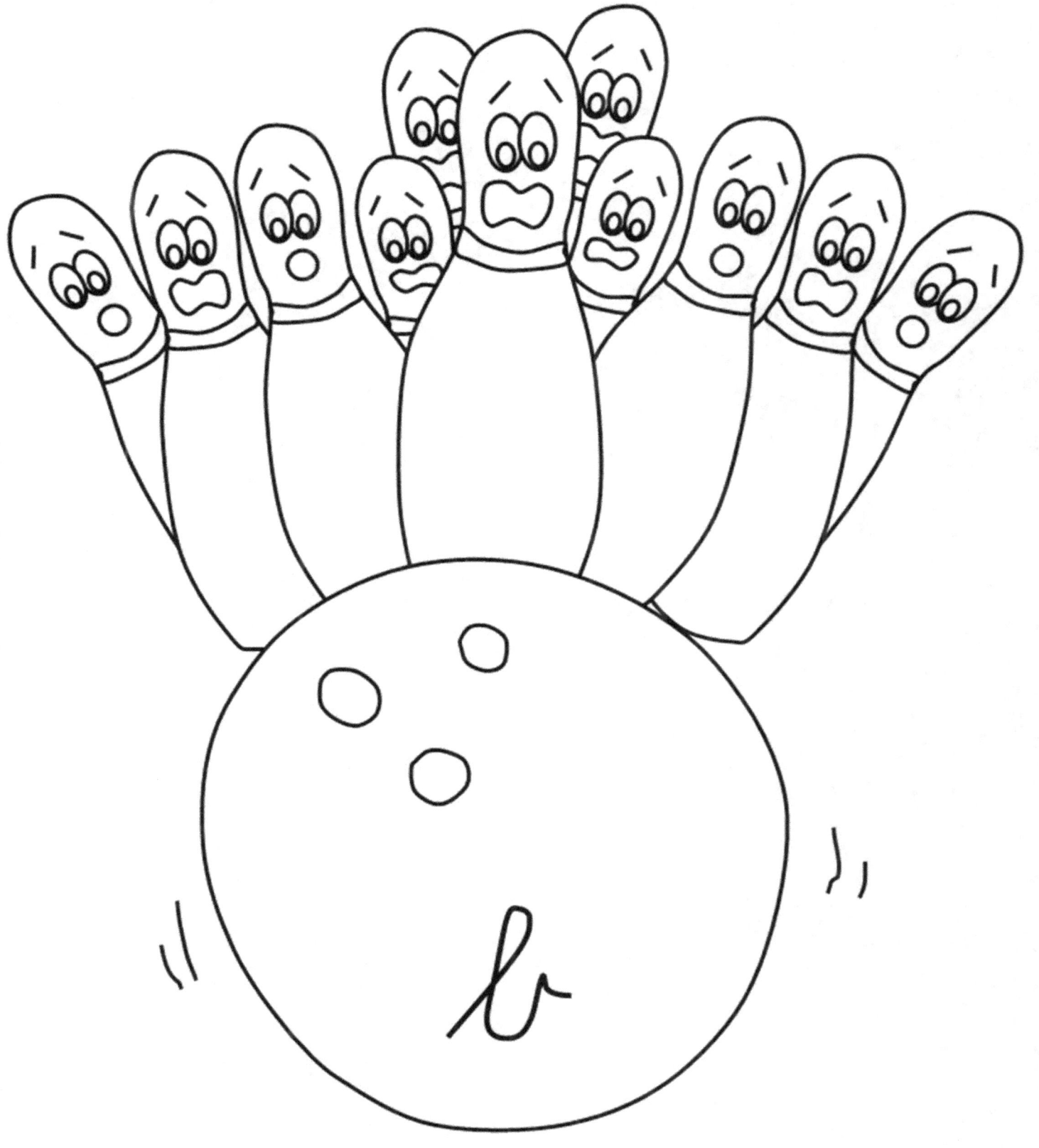

Trace the steps for making the letter b on the following line.

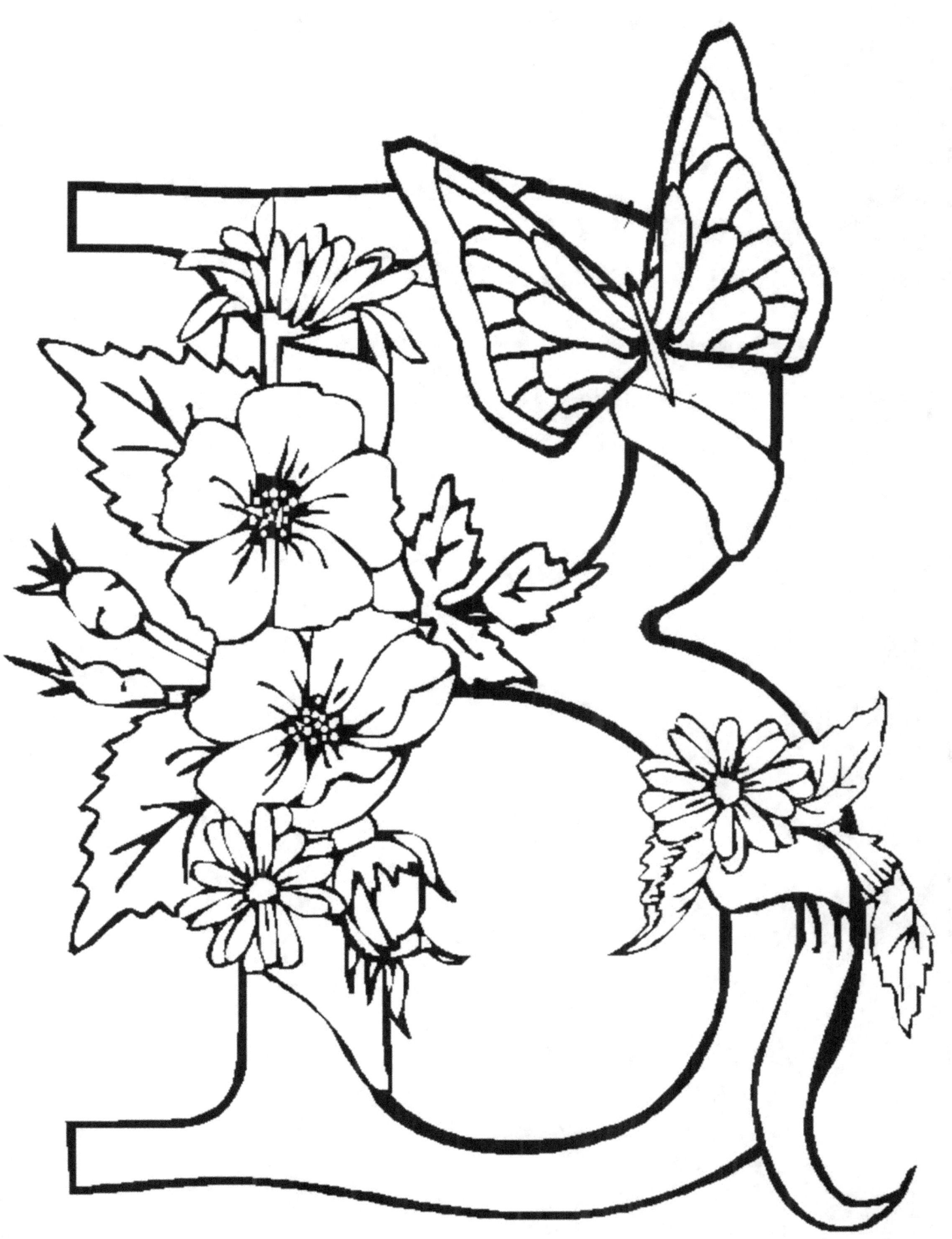

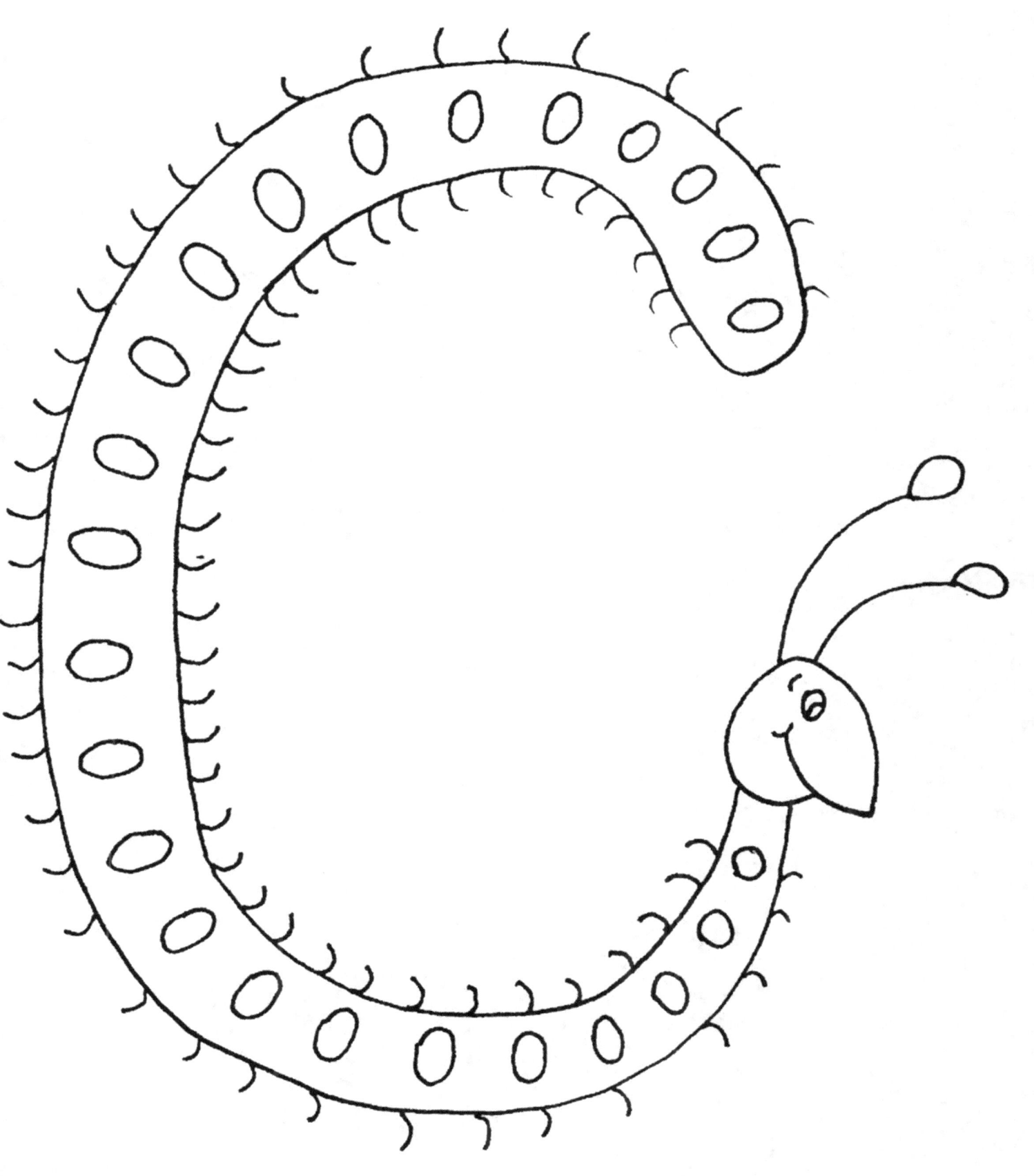

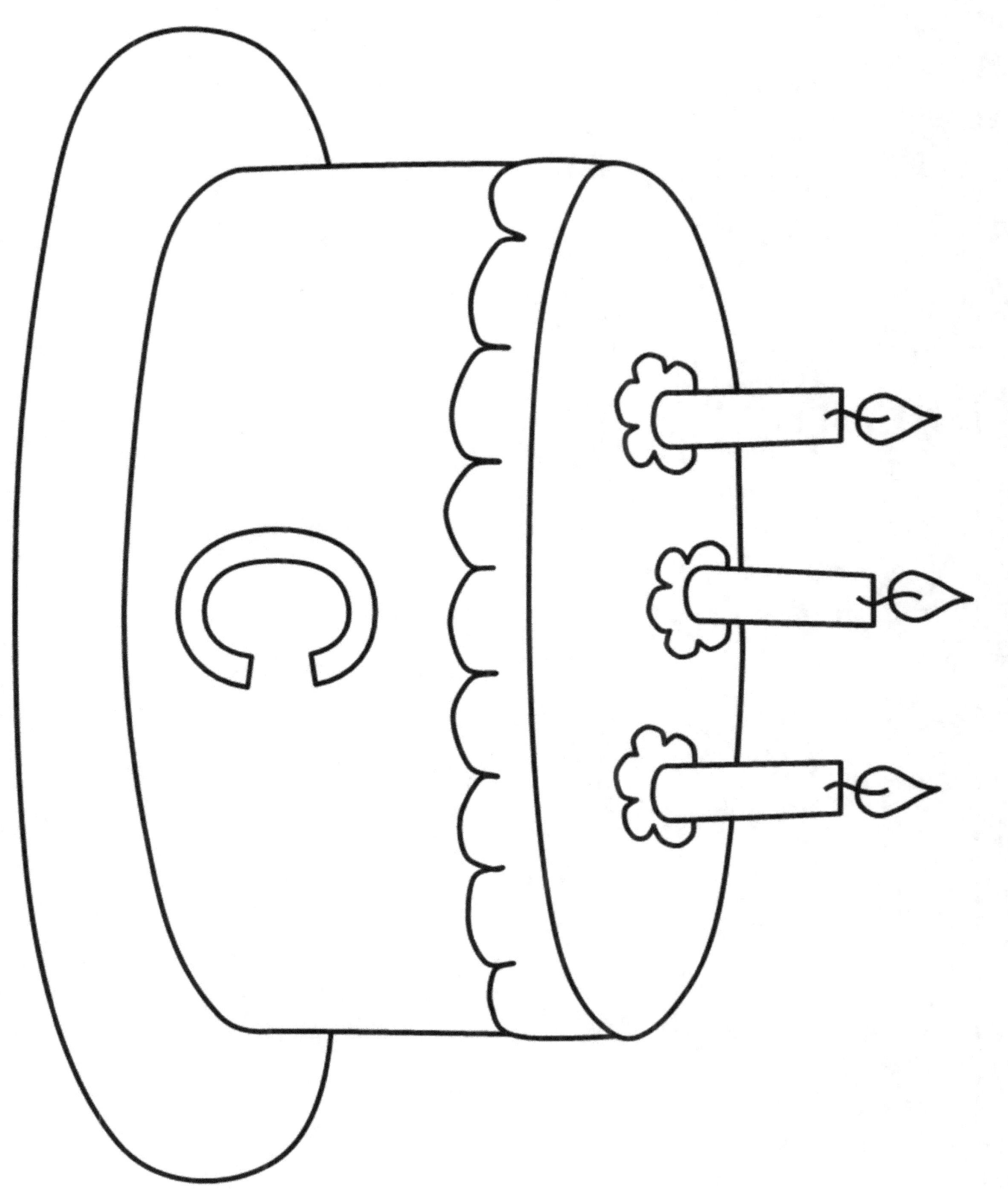

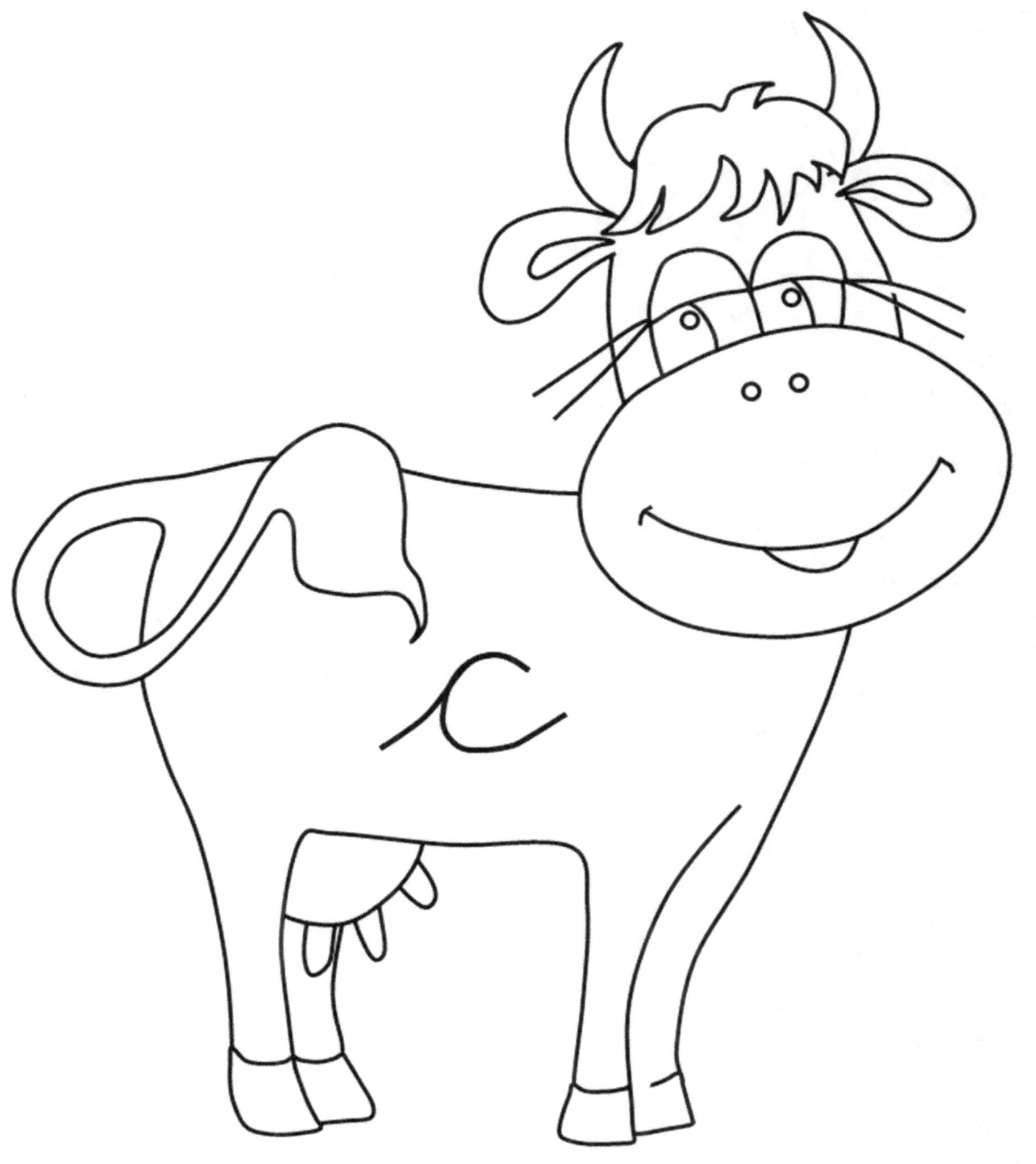

Trace the steps for making the letter c on the following line.

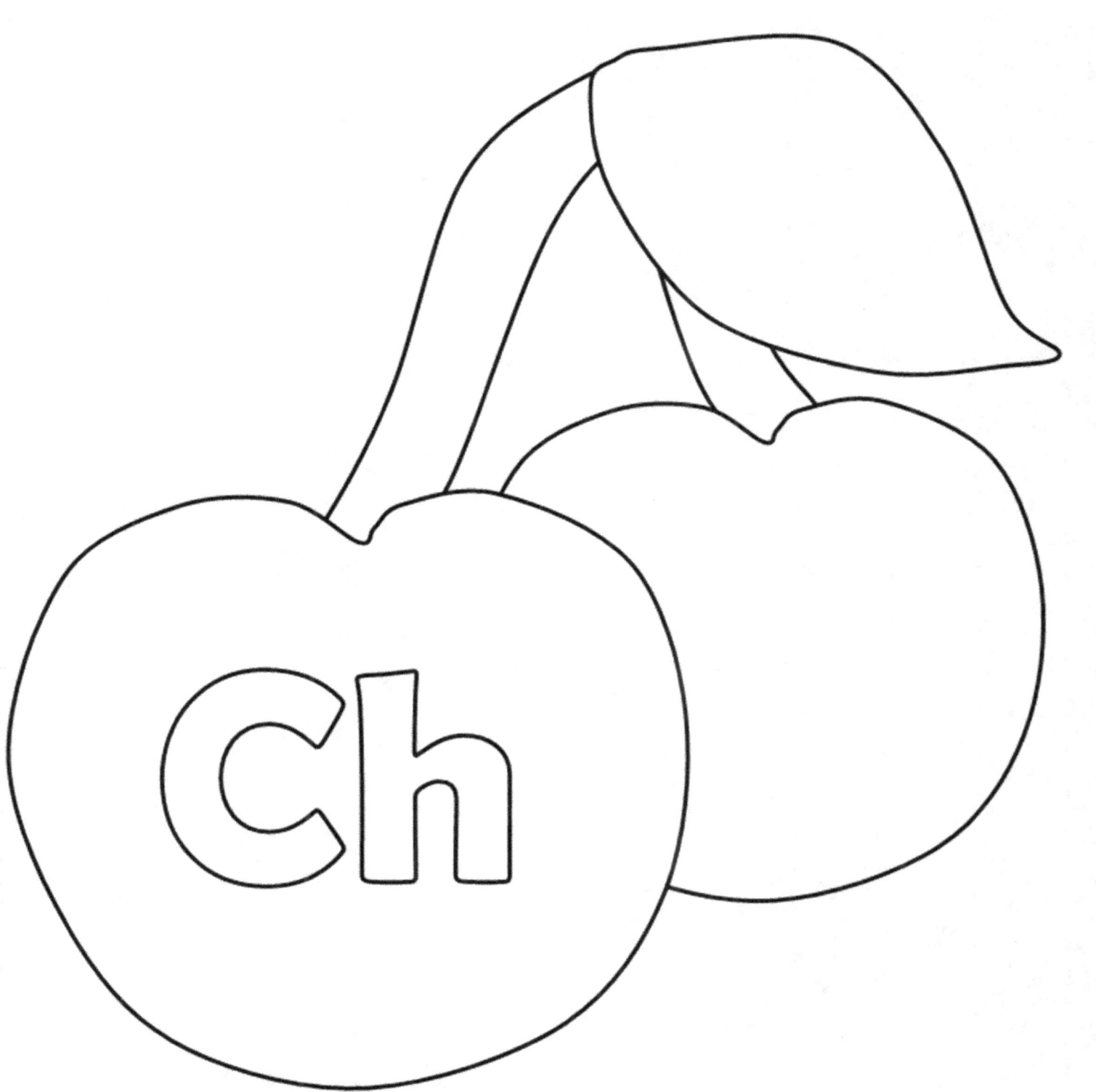

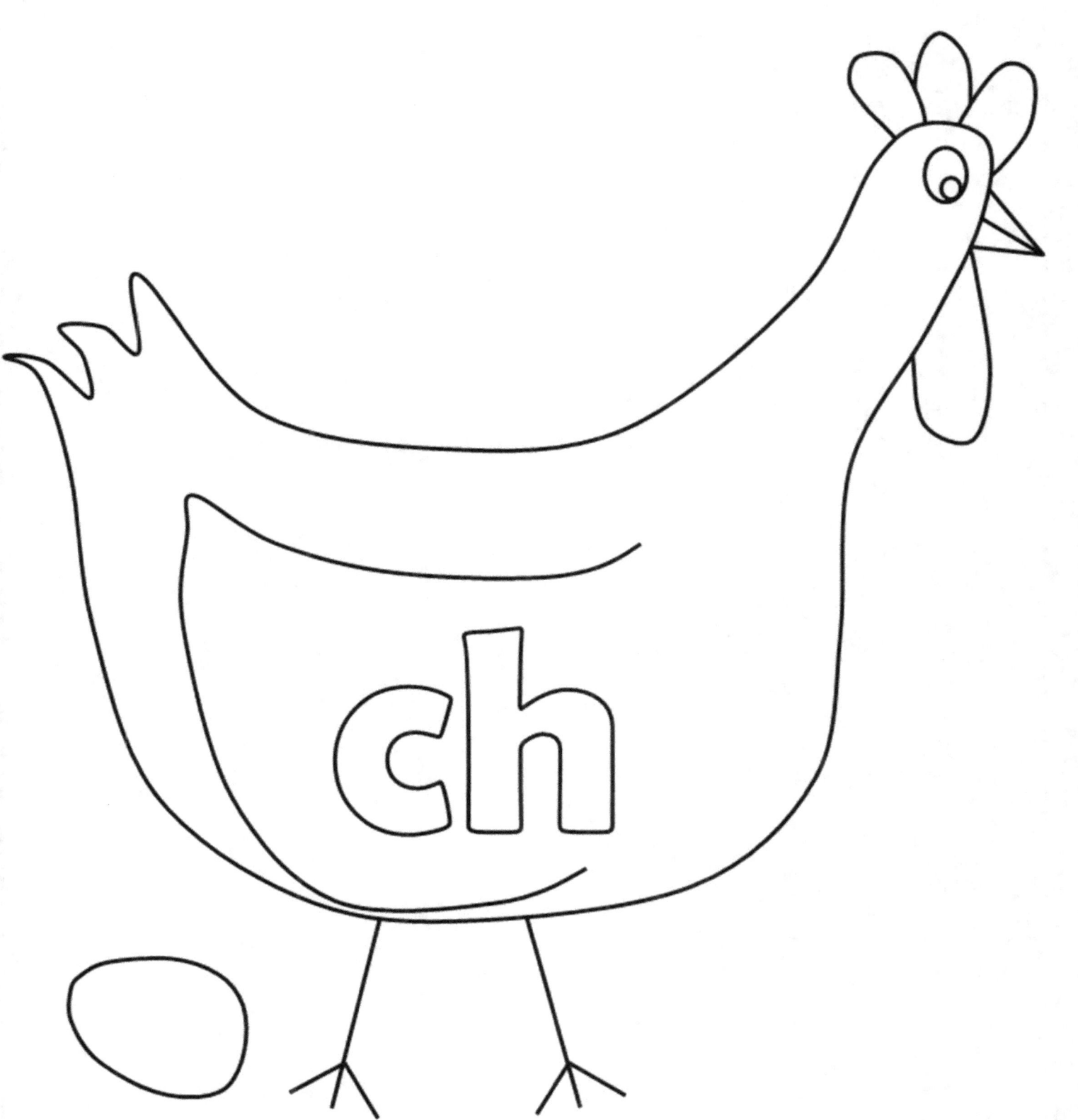

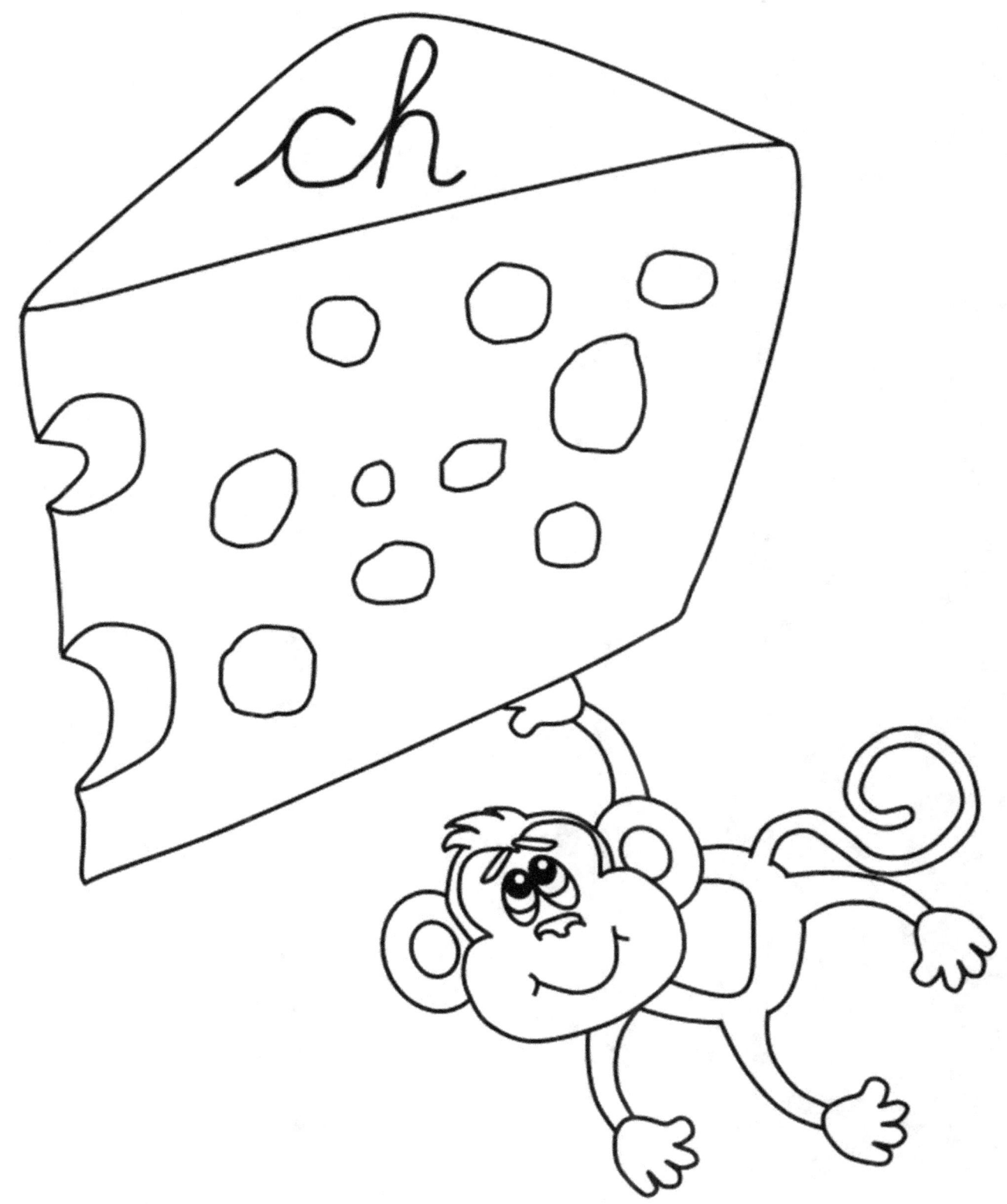

Trace the steps for making the letter c on the following line.

c   h   ch   ch   ch   ch

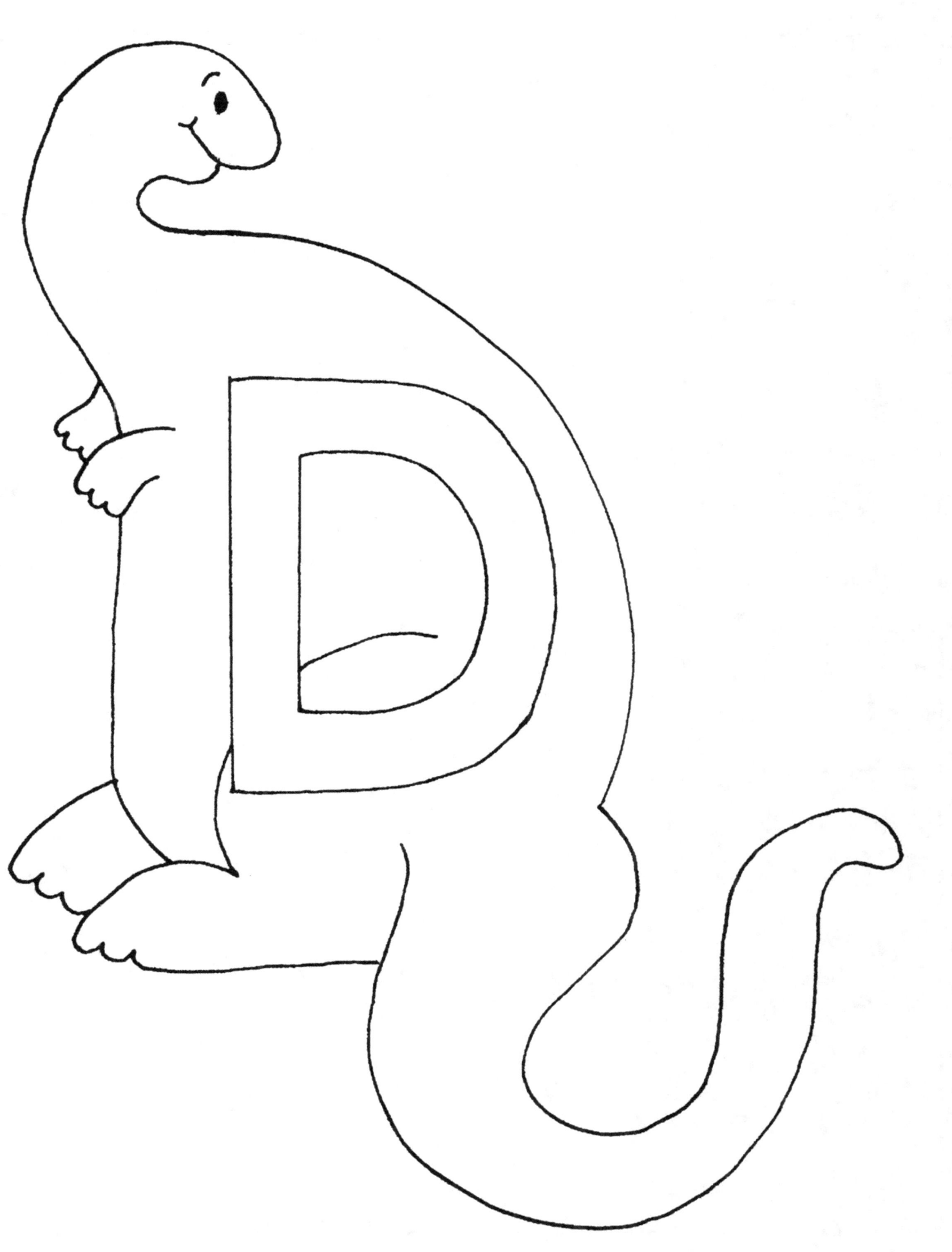

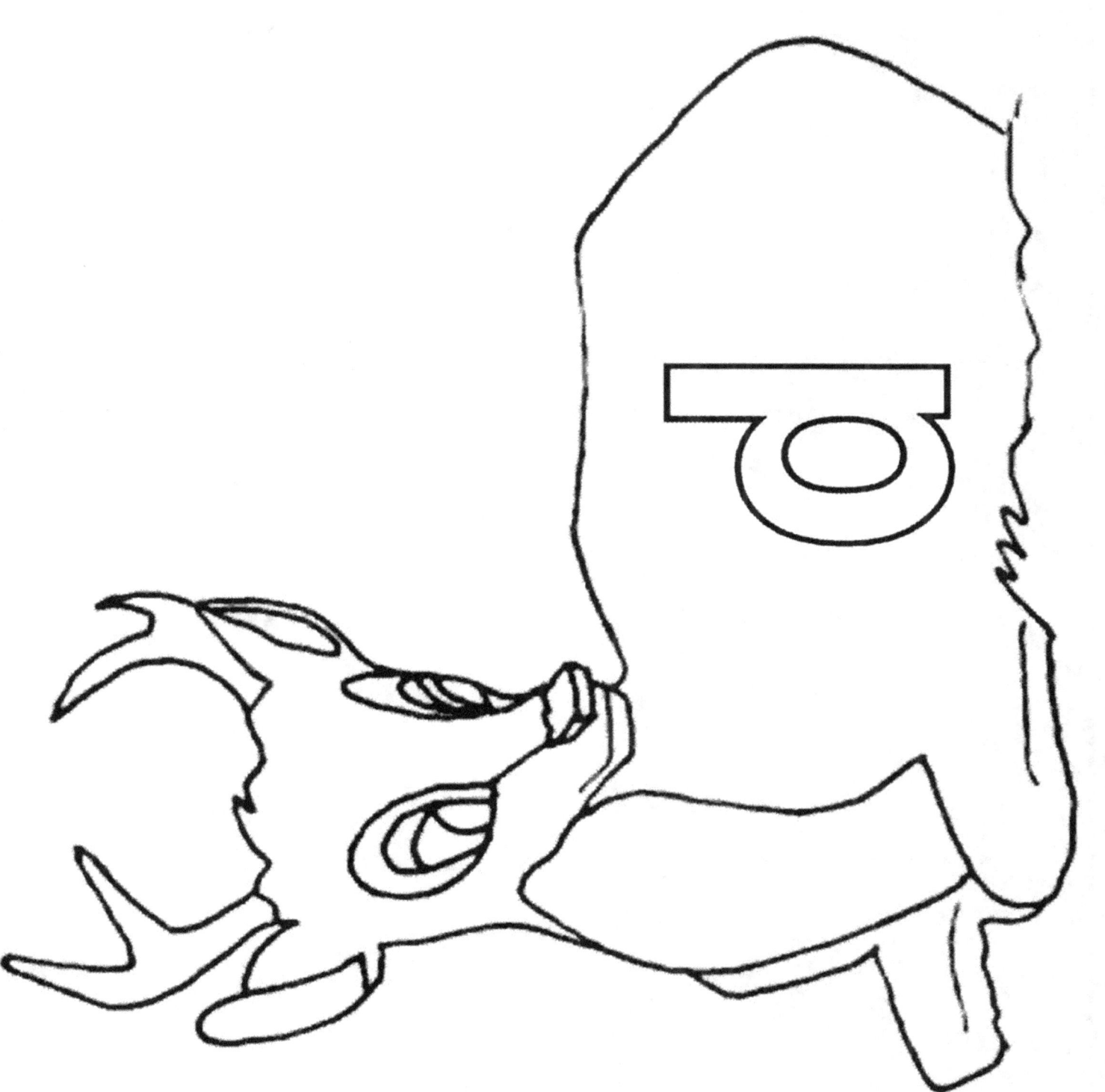

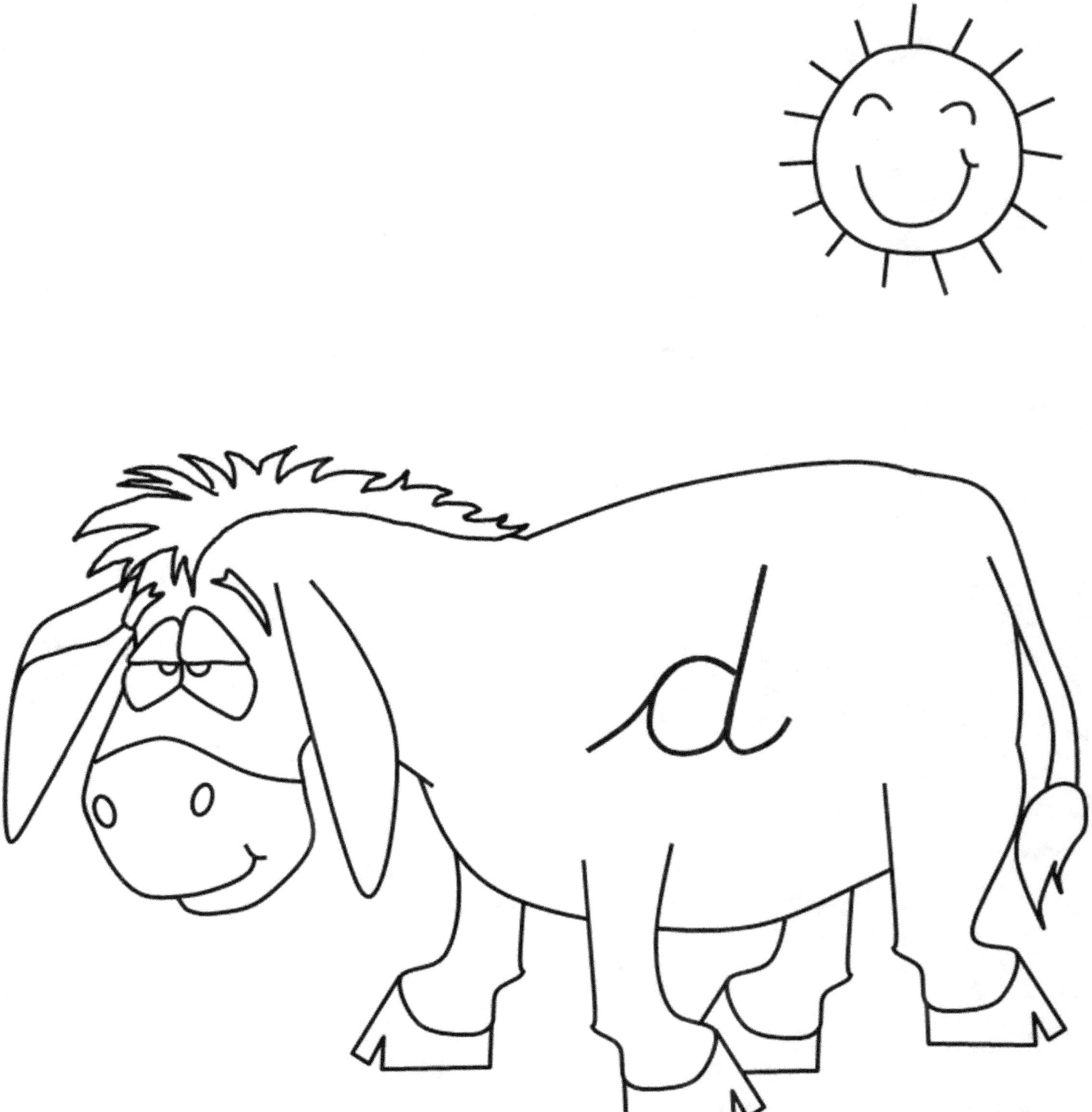

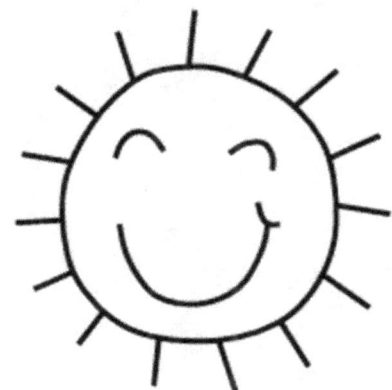

Trace the steps for making the letter d on the following line.

$\mathcal{d}$ $\mathcal{d}$ $\mathcal{d}$ $\mathcal{d}$ $\mathcal{dd}$

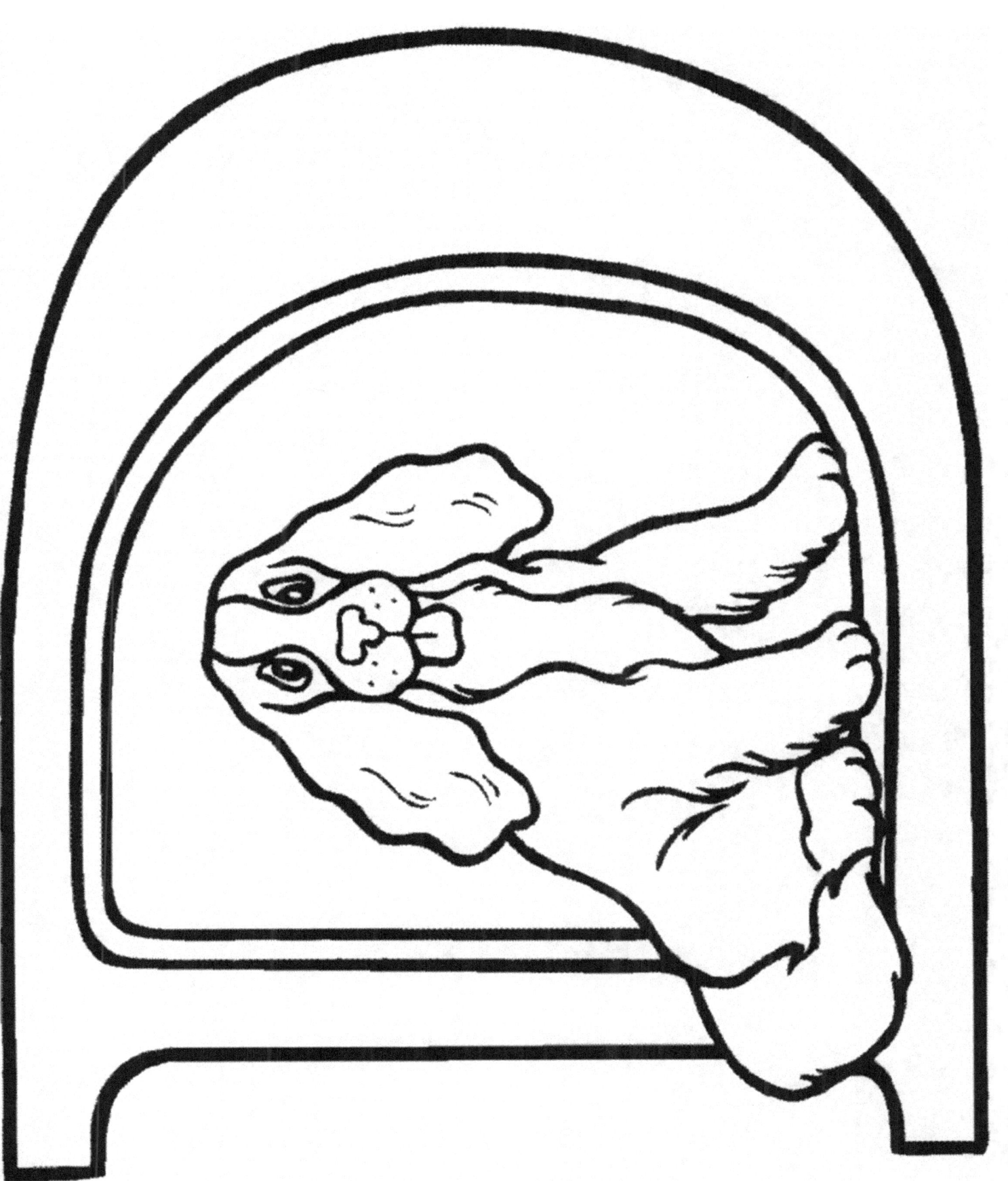

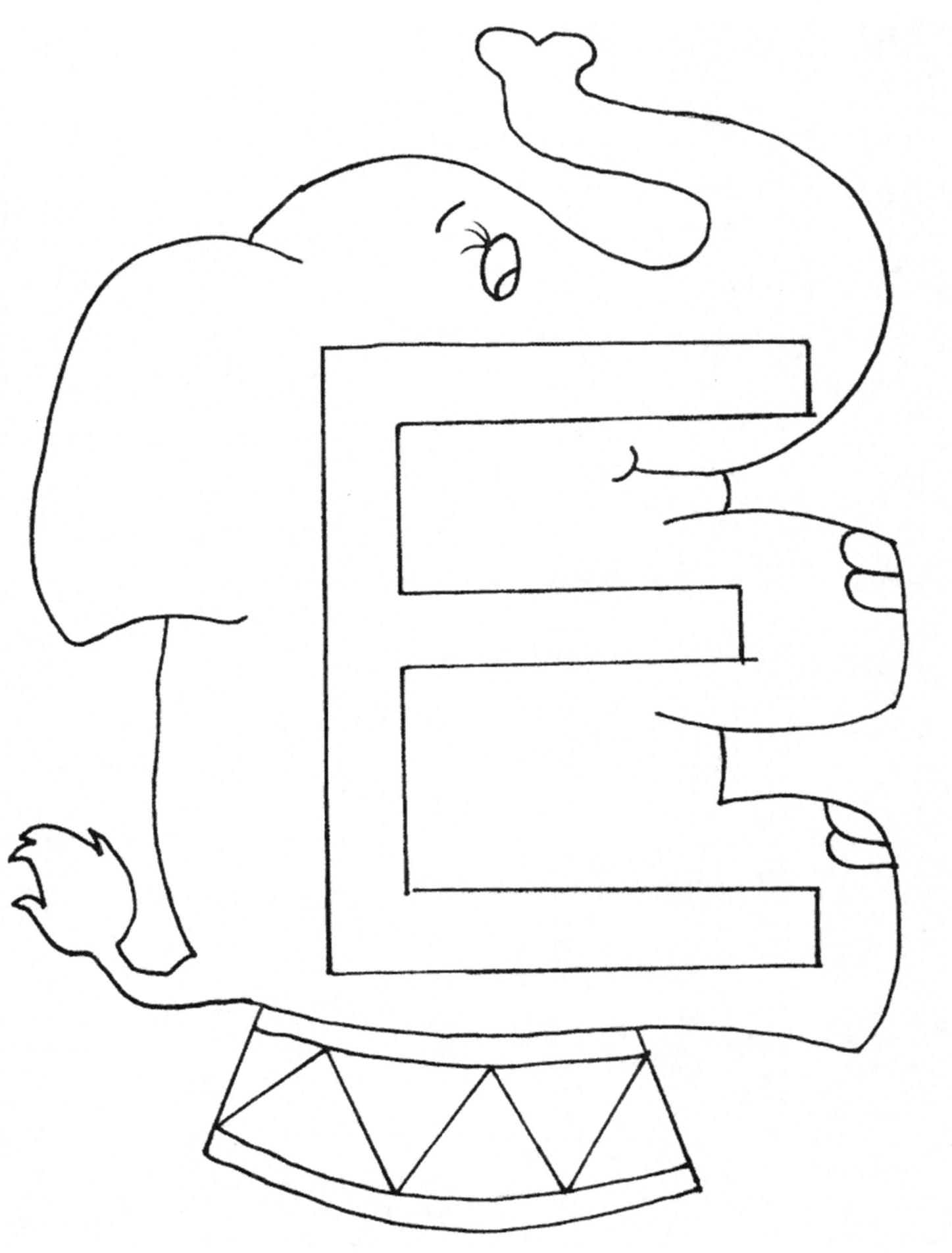

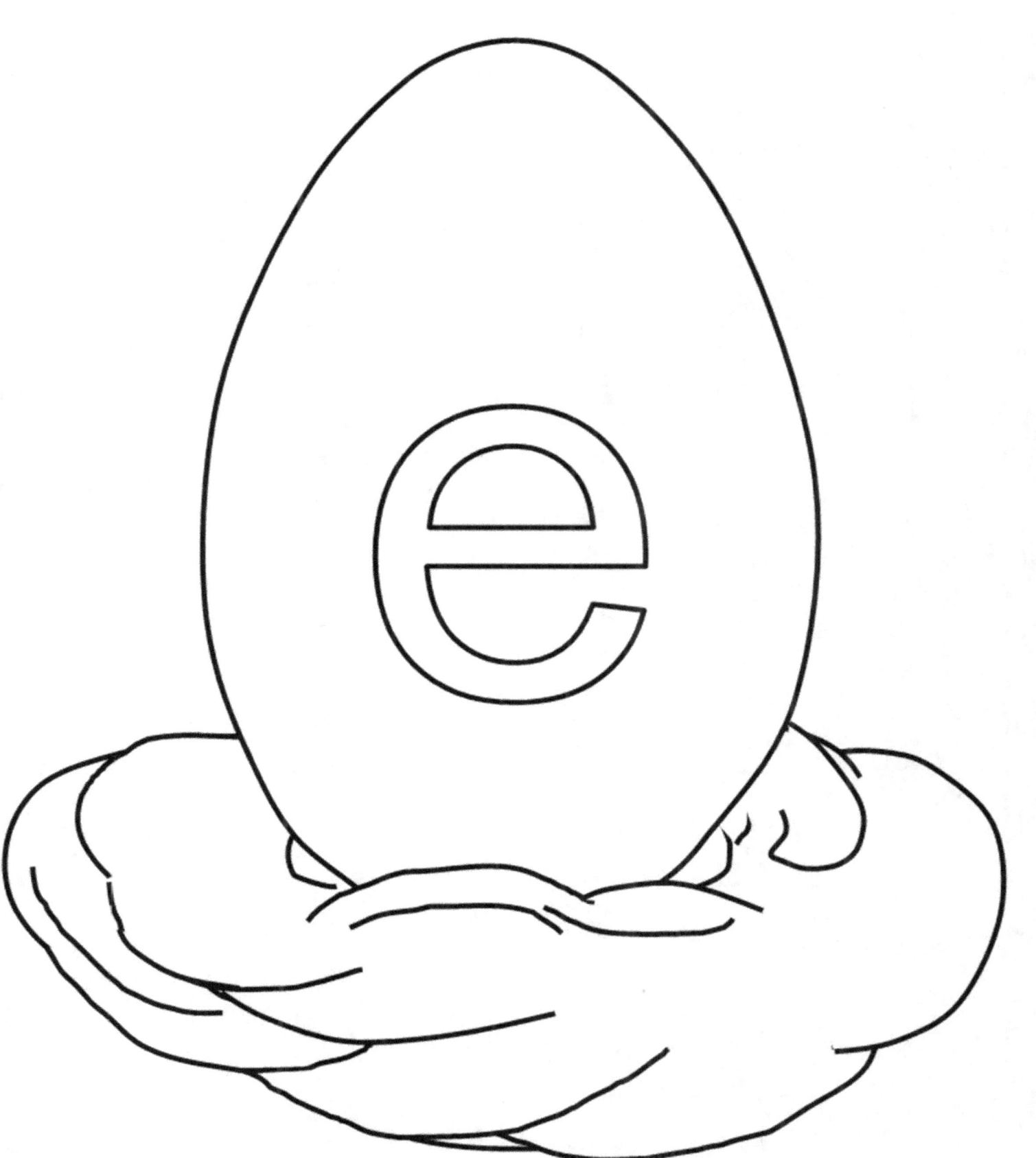

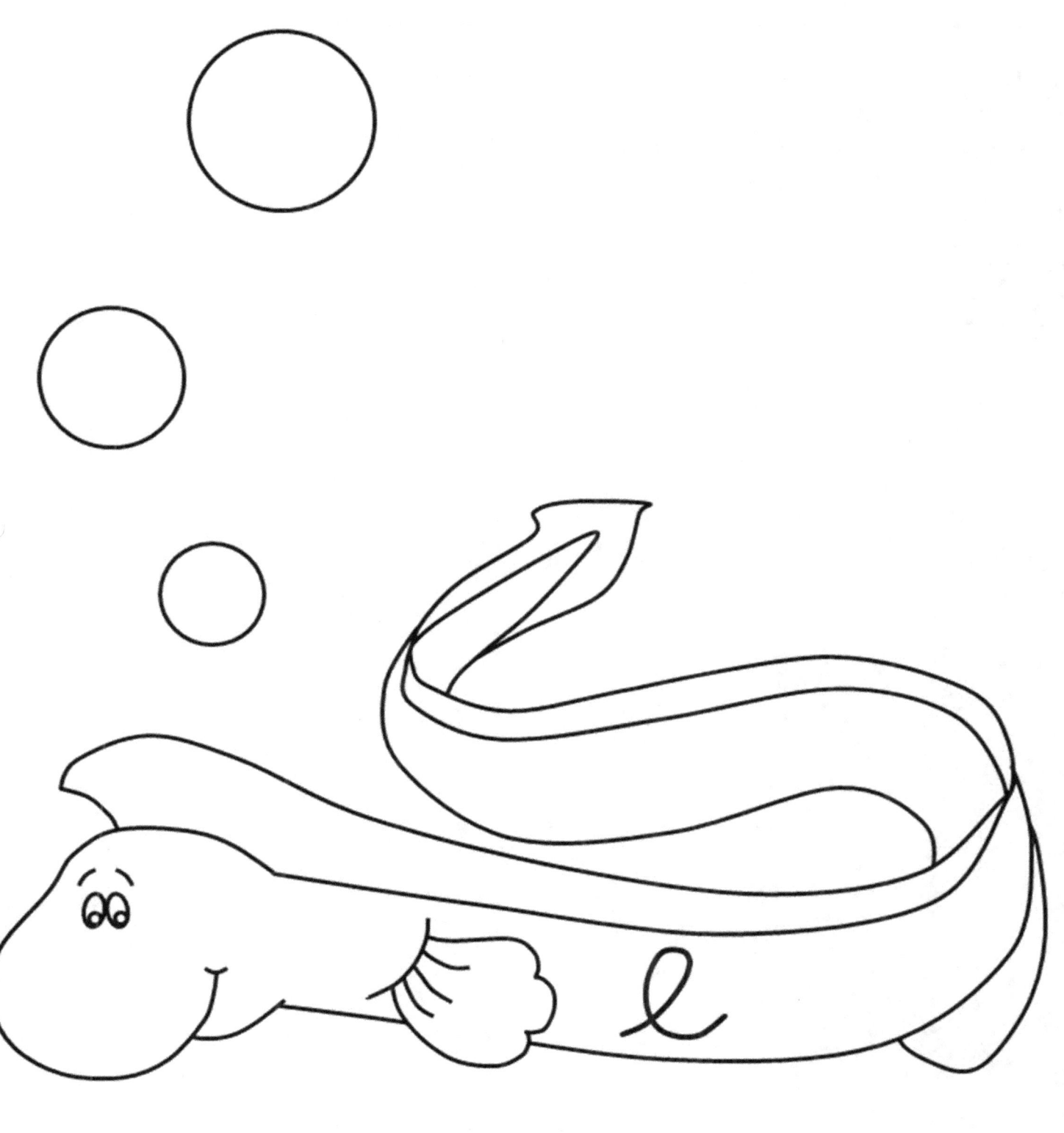

Trace the steps for making the letter e on the following line.

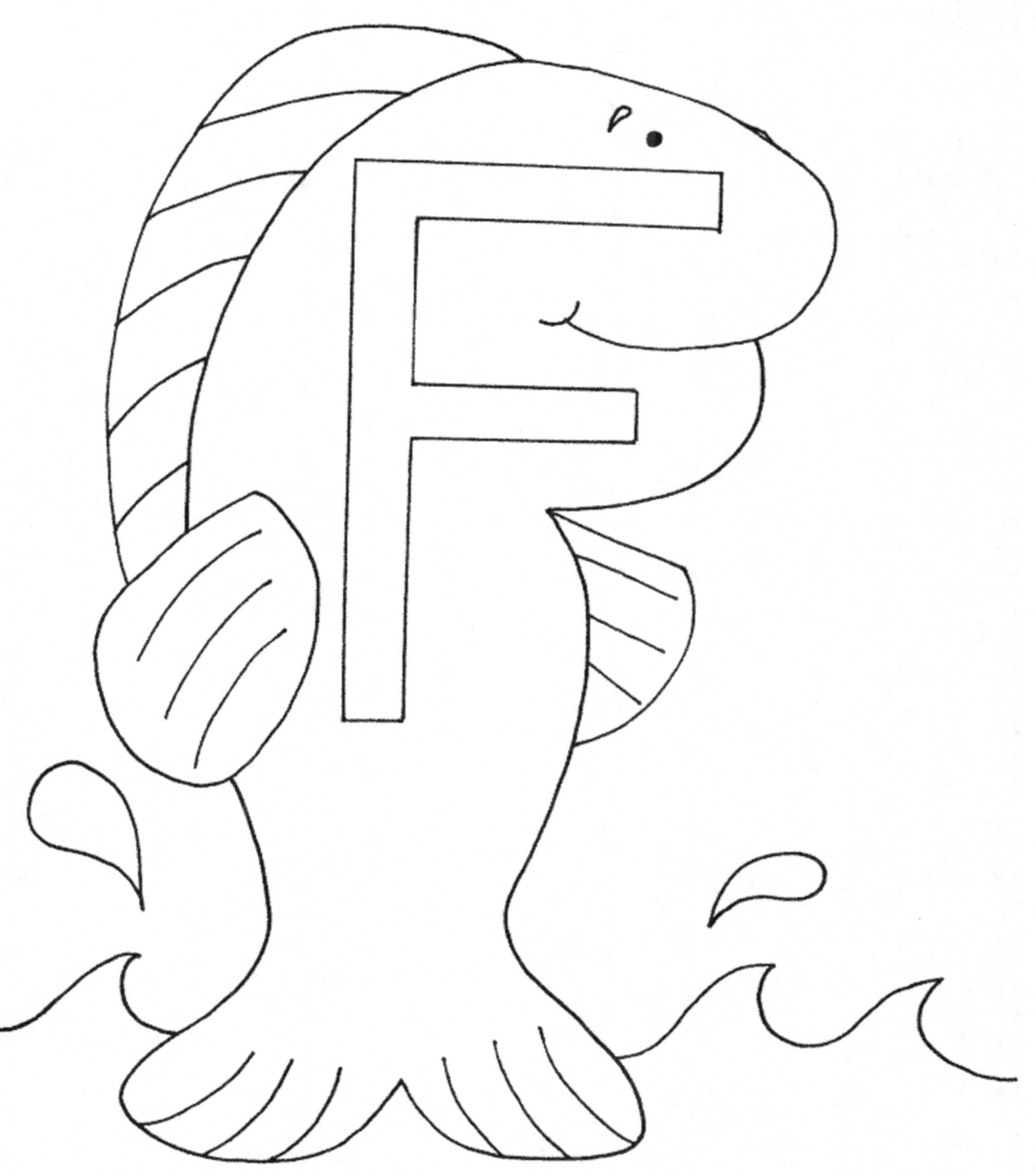

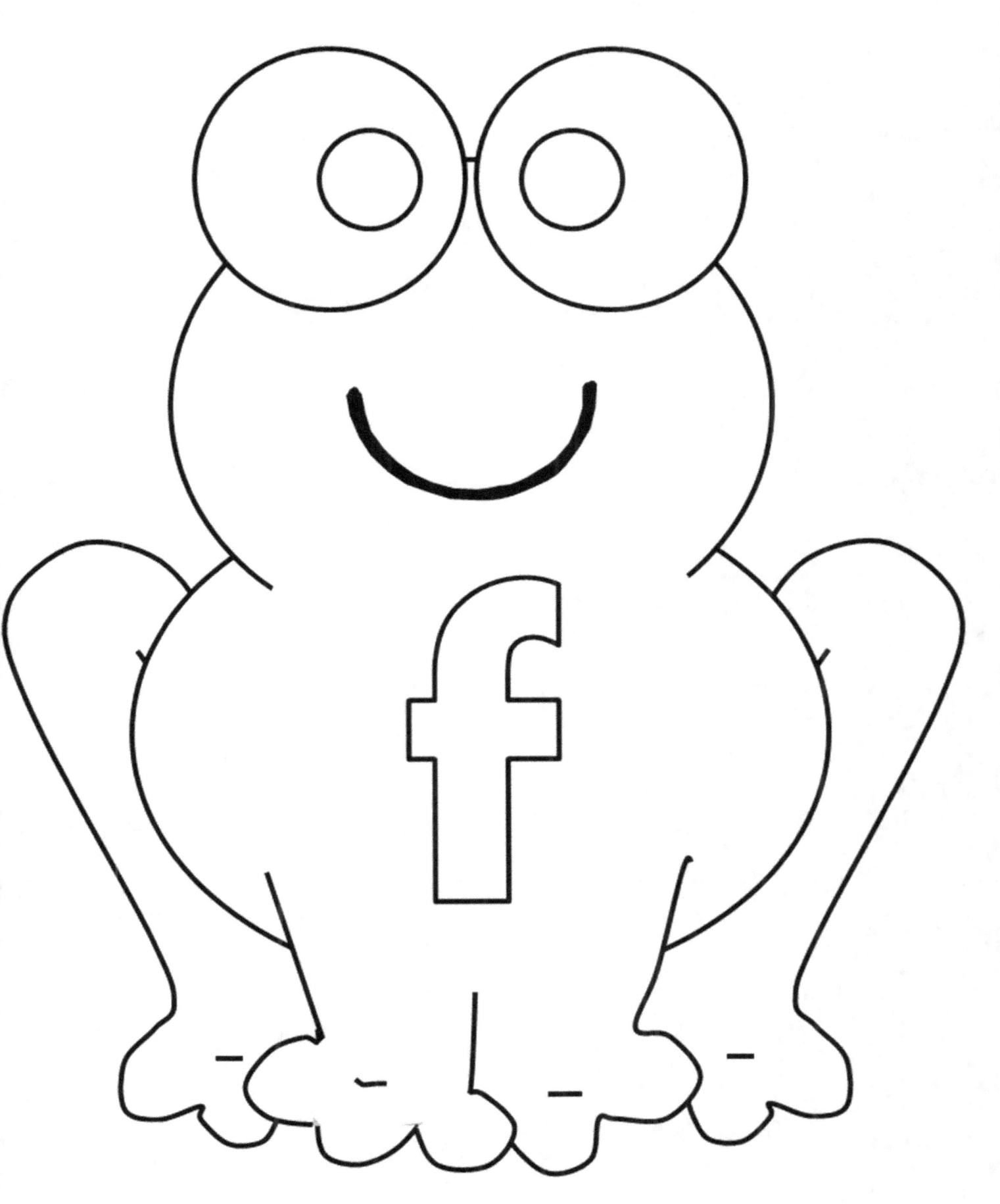

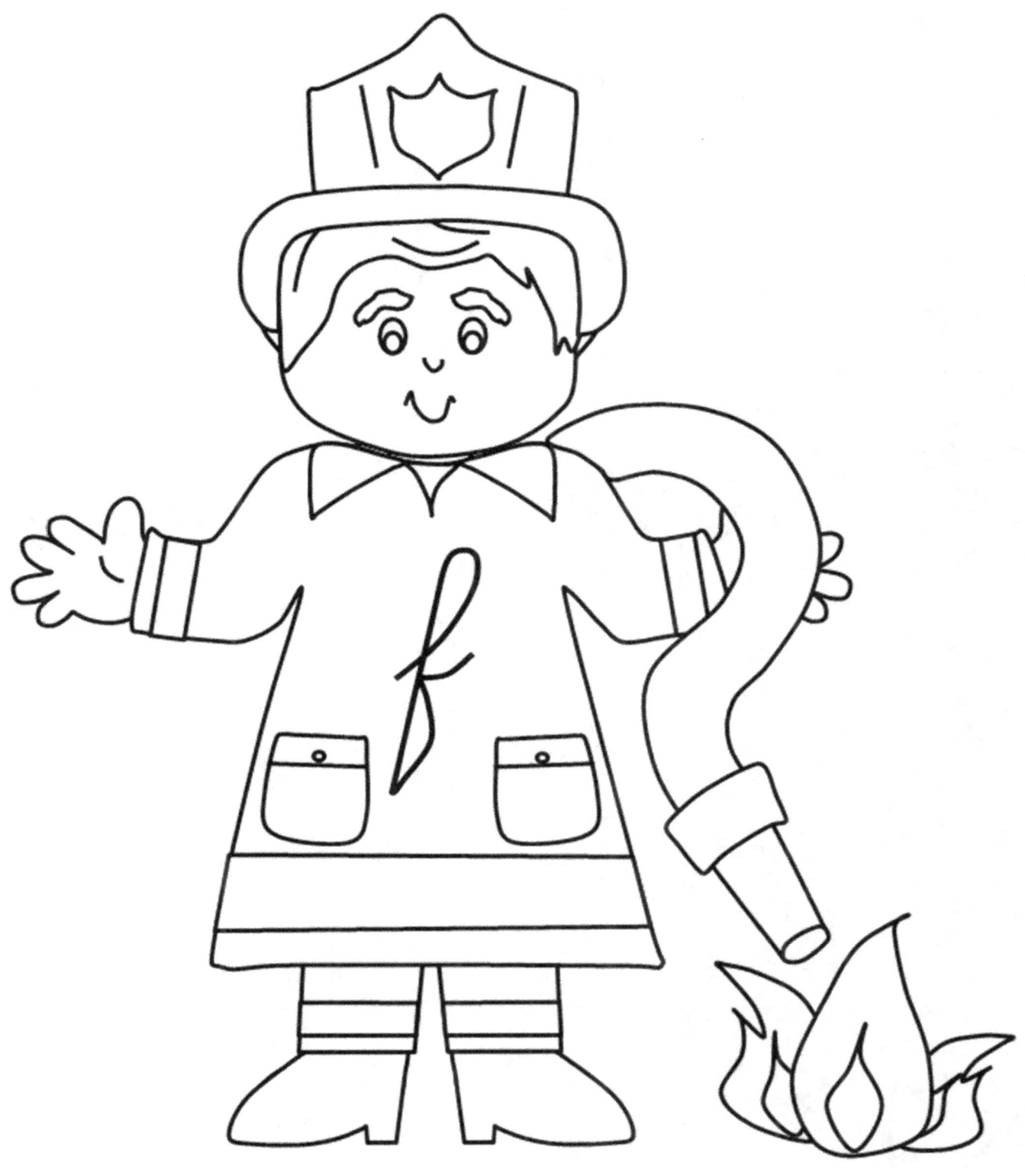

Trace the steps for making the letter f on the following line.

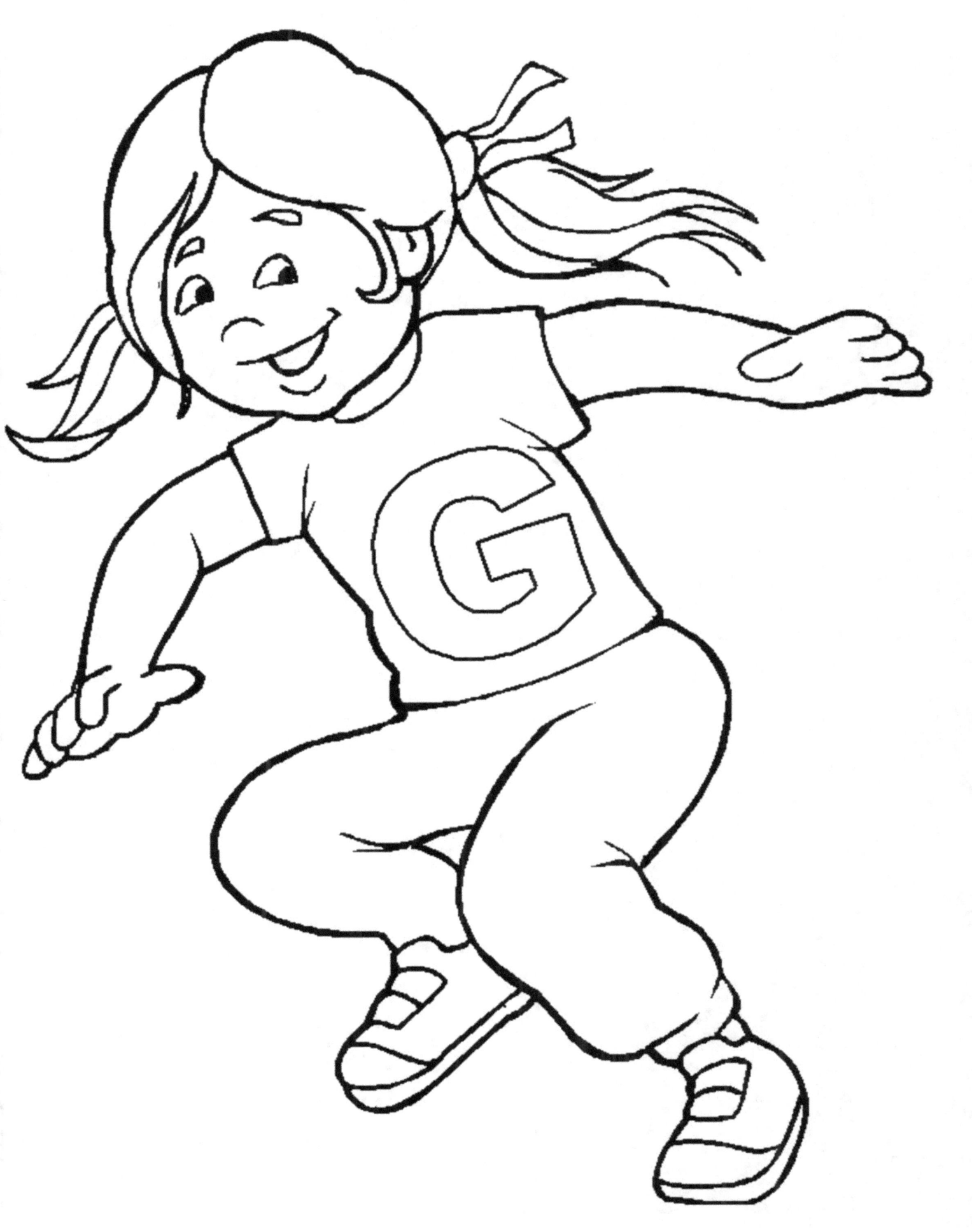

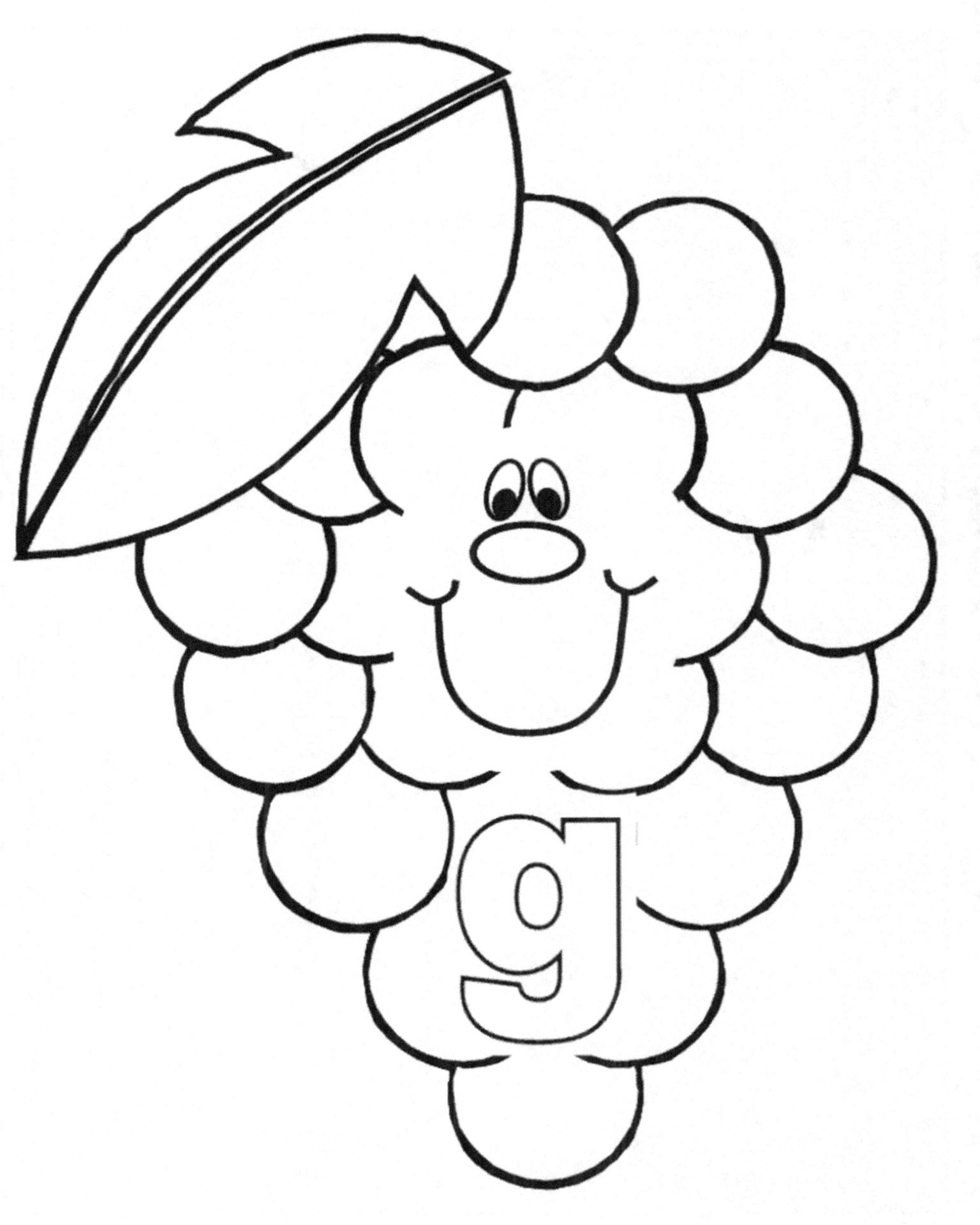

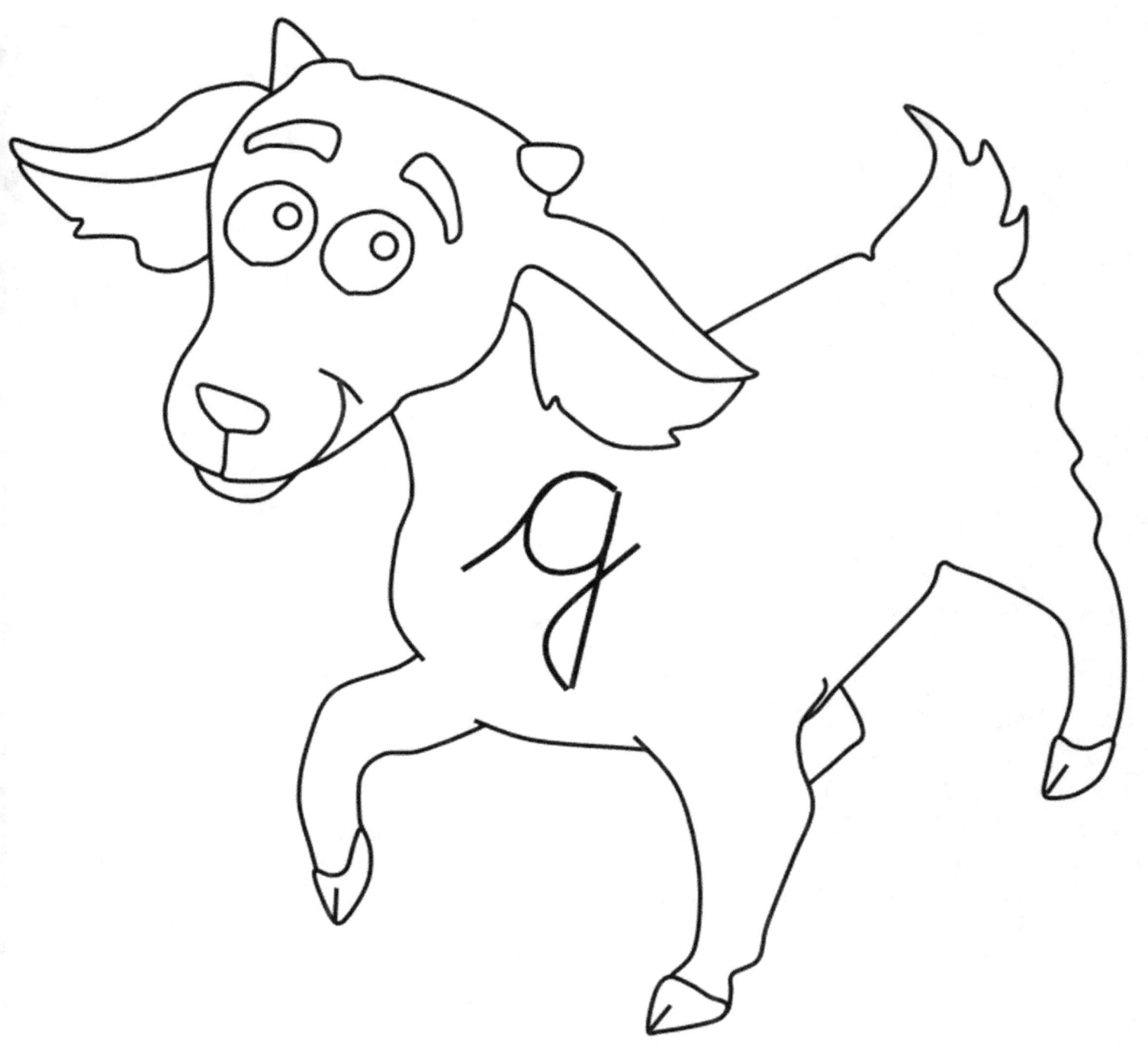

Trace the steps for making the letter g on the following line.

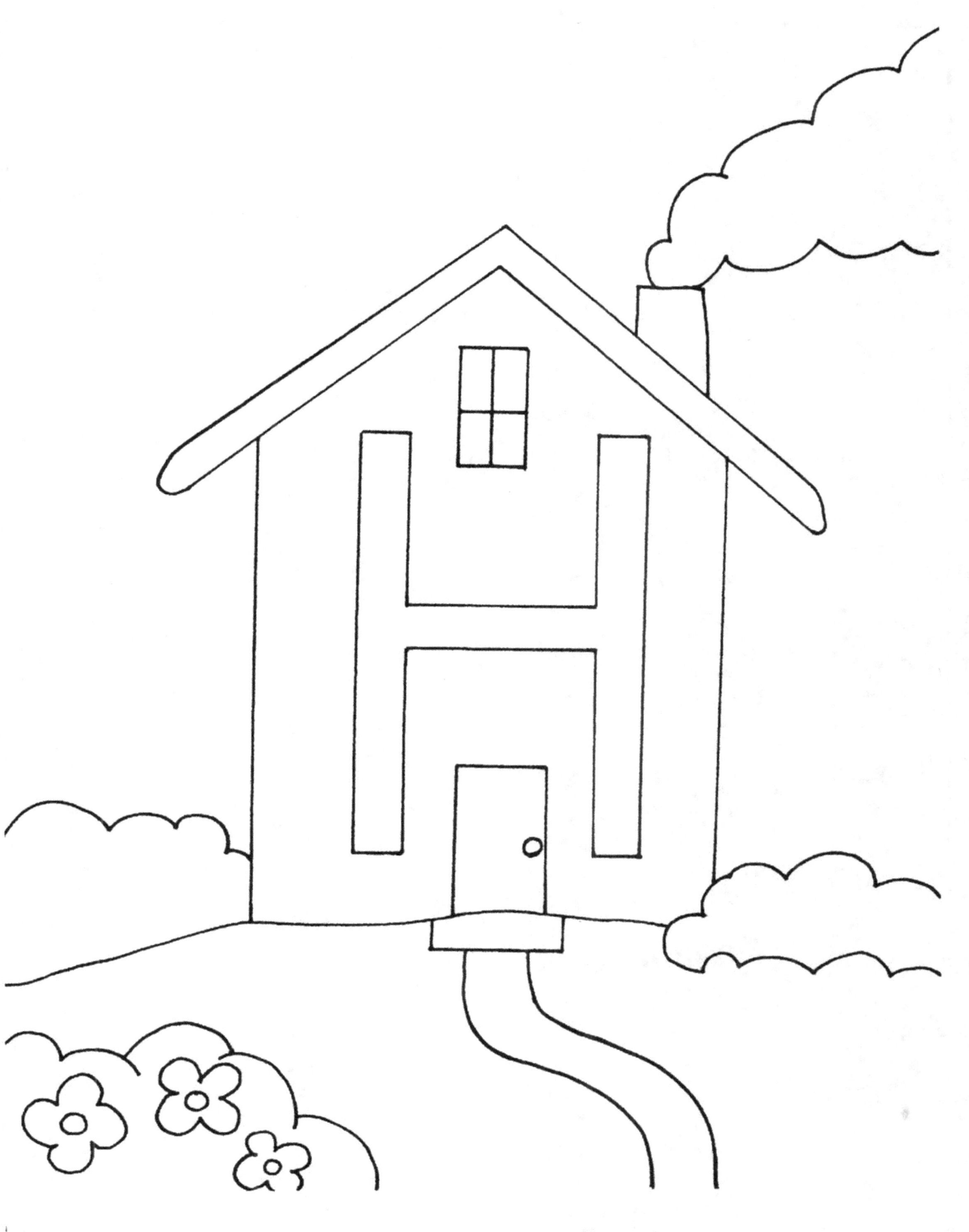

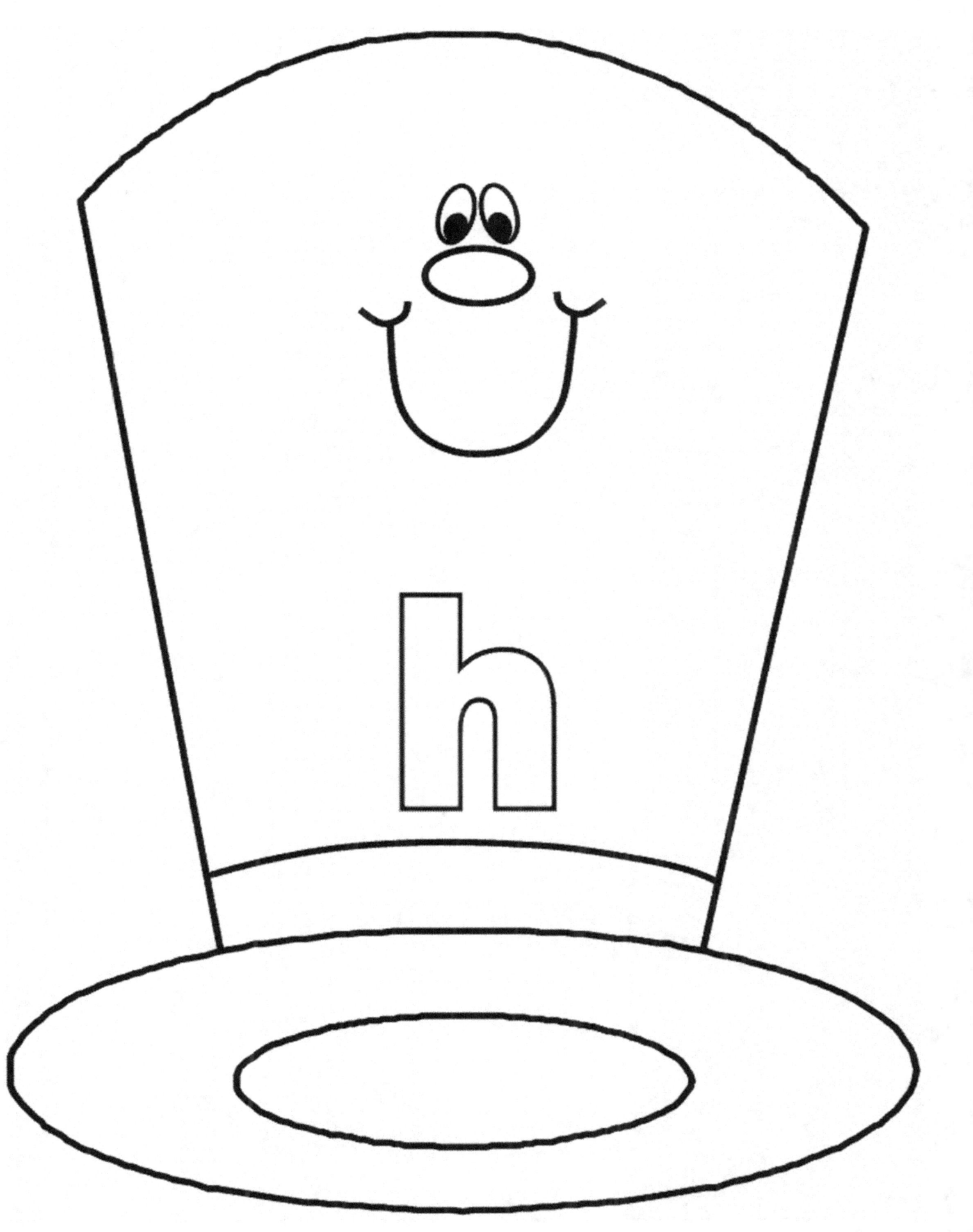

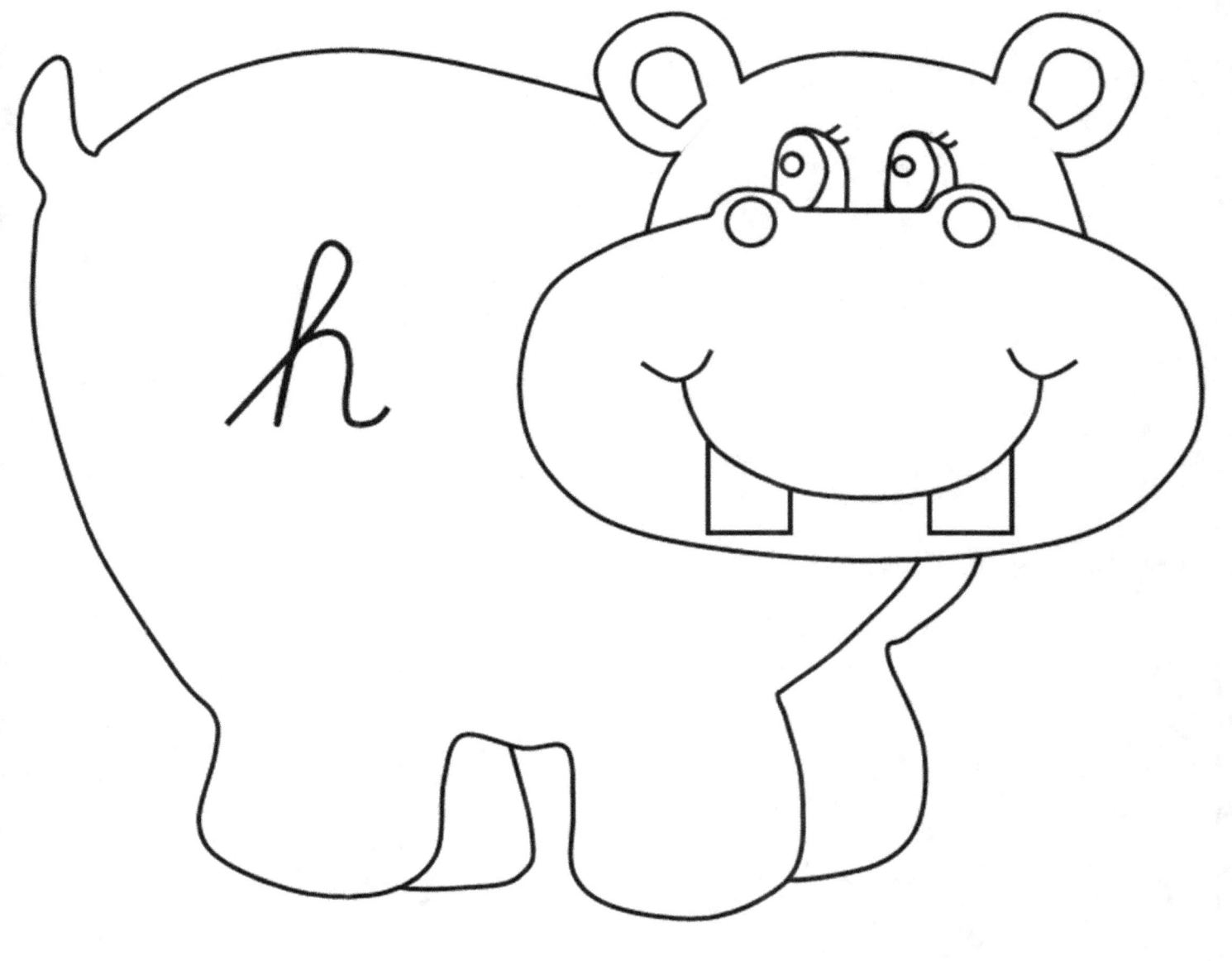

Trace the steps for making the letter h on the following line.

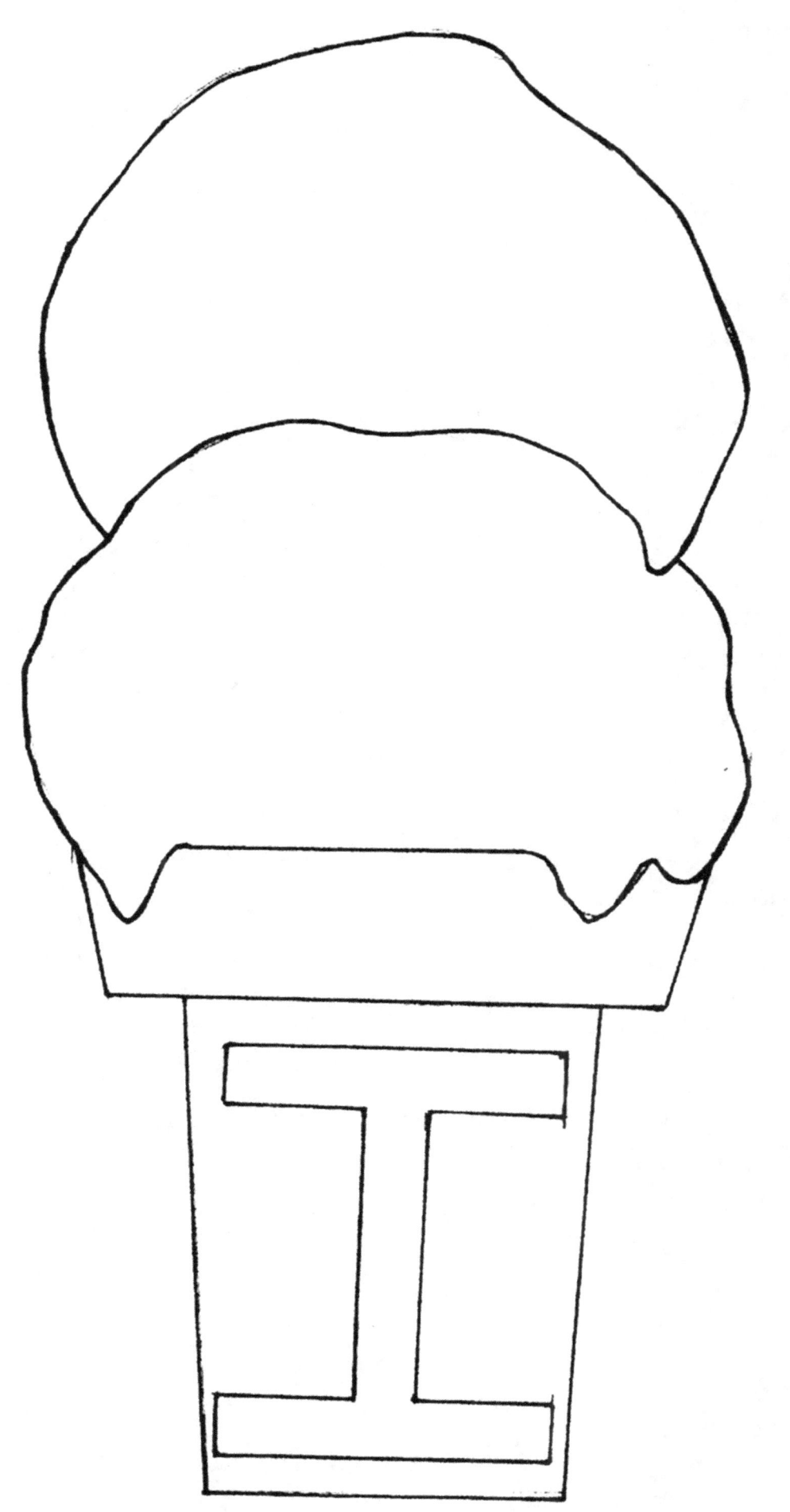

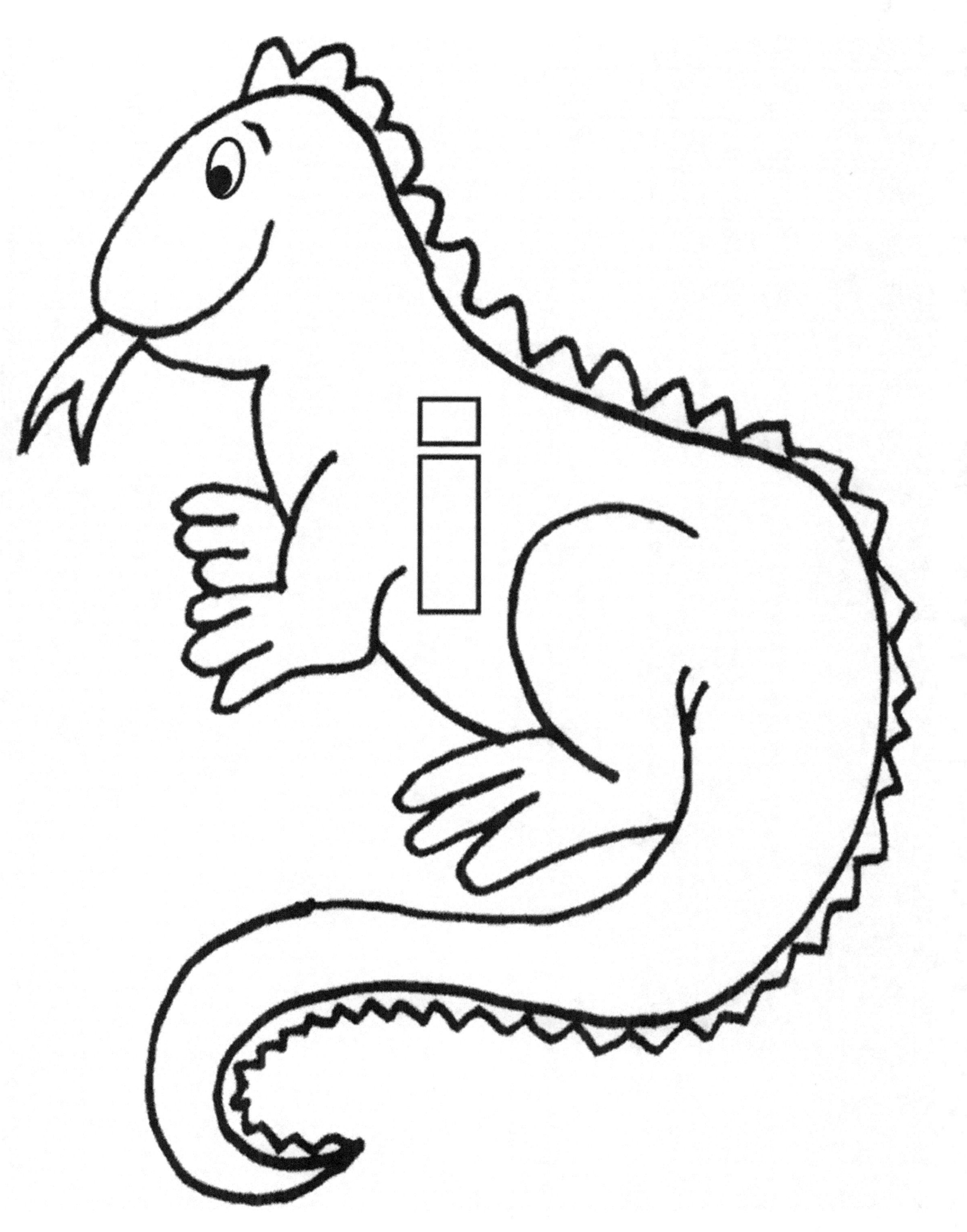

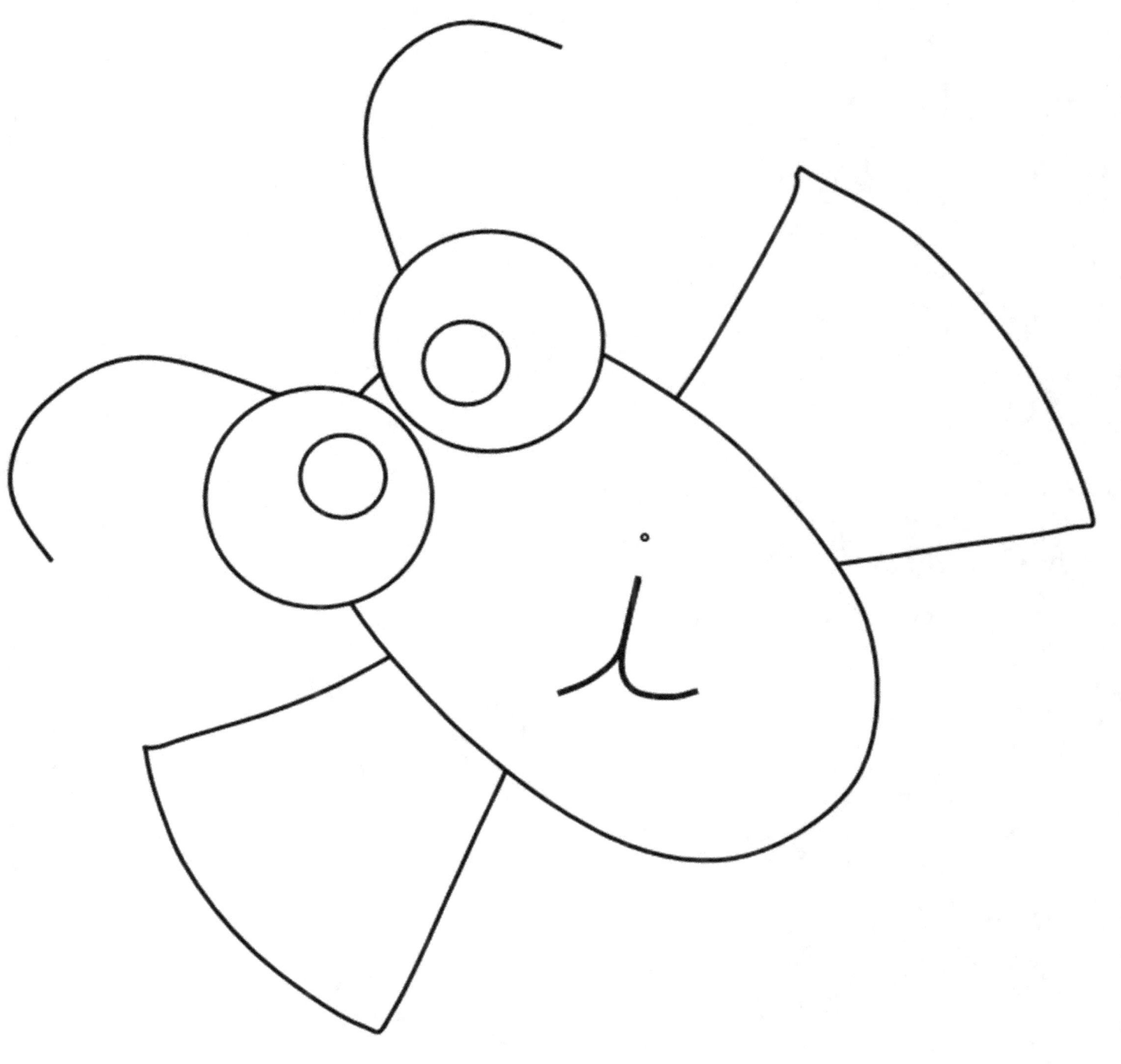

Trace the steps for making the letter i on the following line.

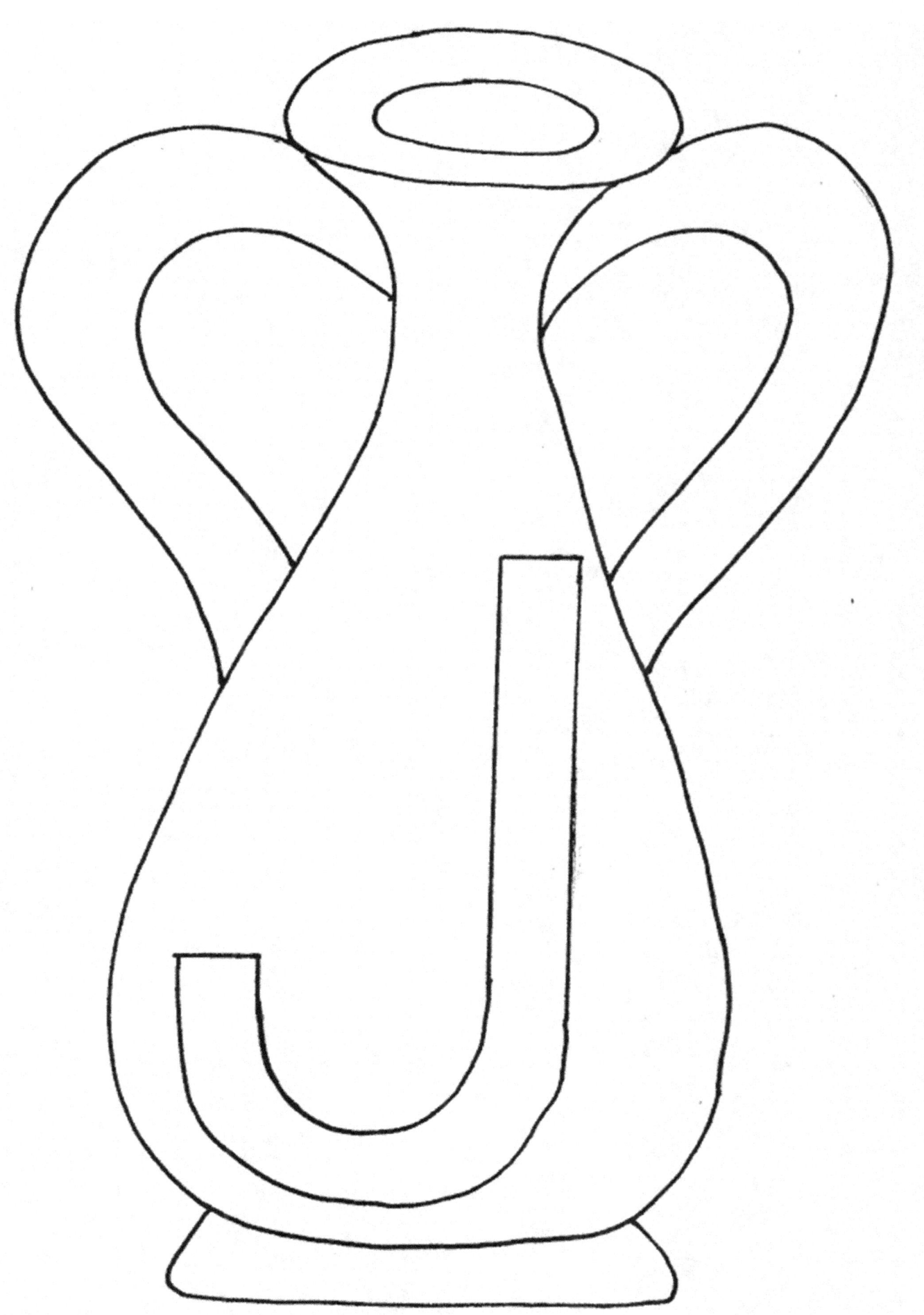

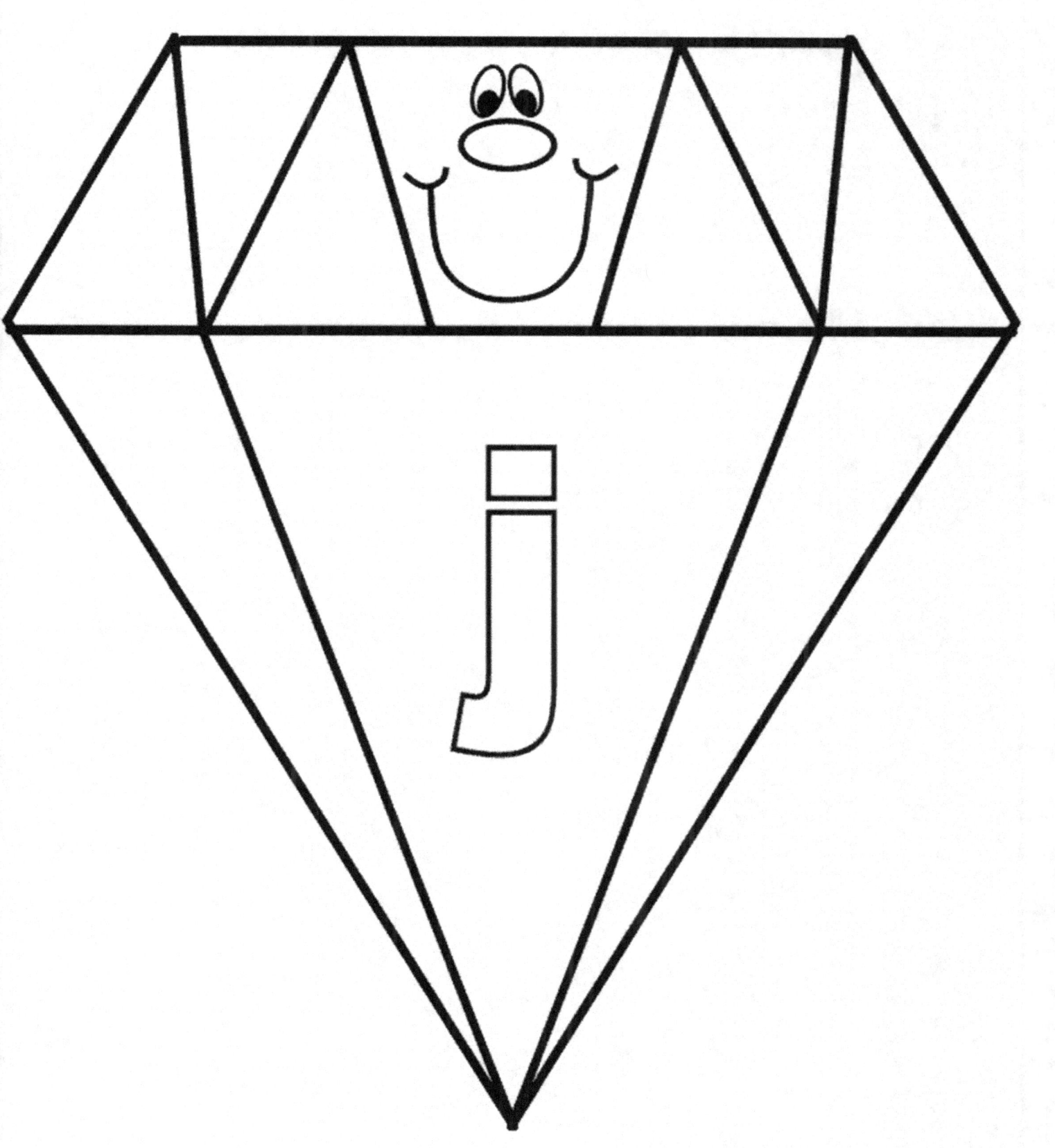

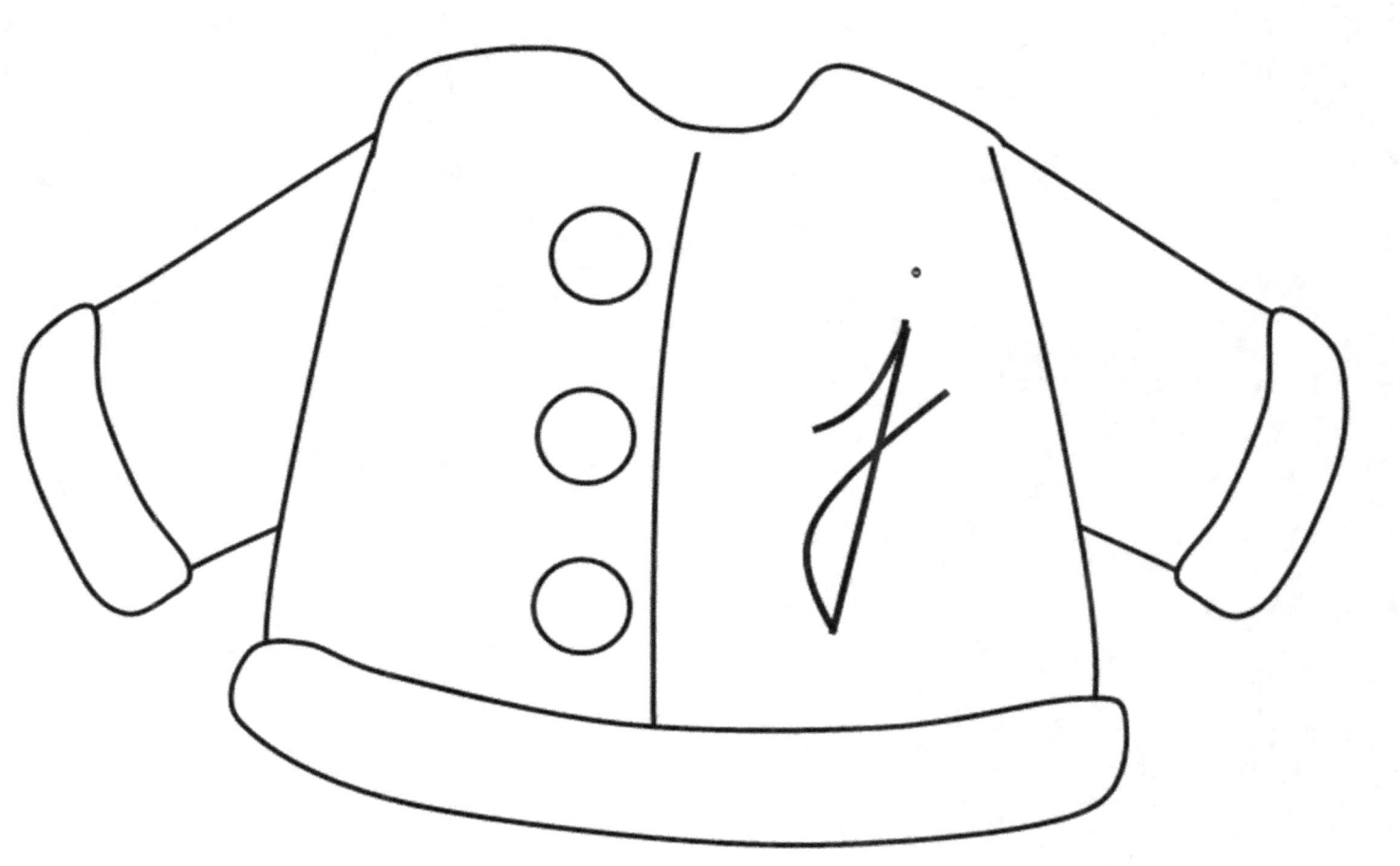

Trace the steps for making the letter j on the following line.

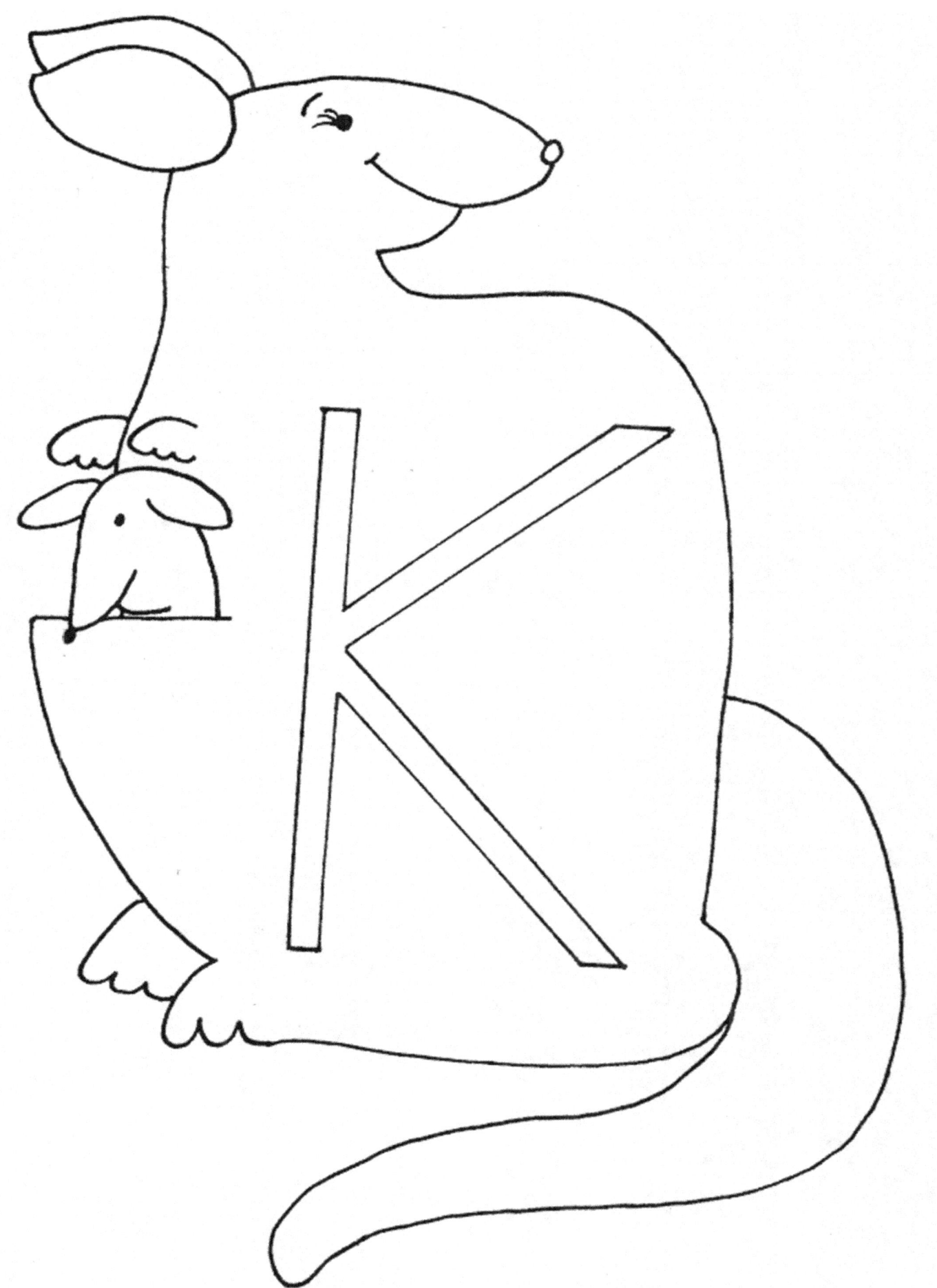

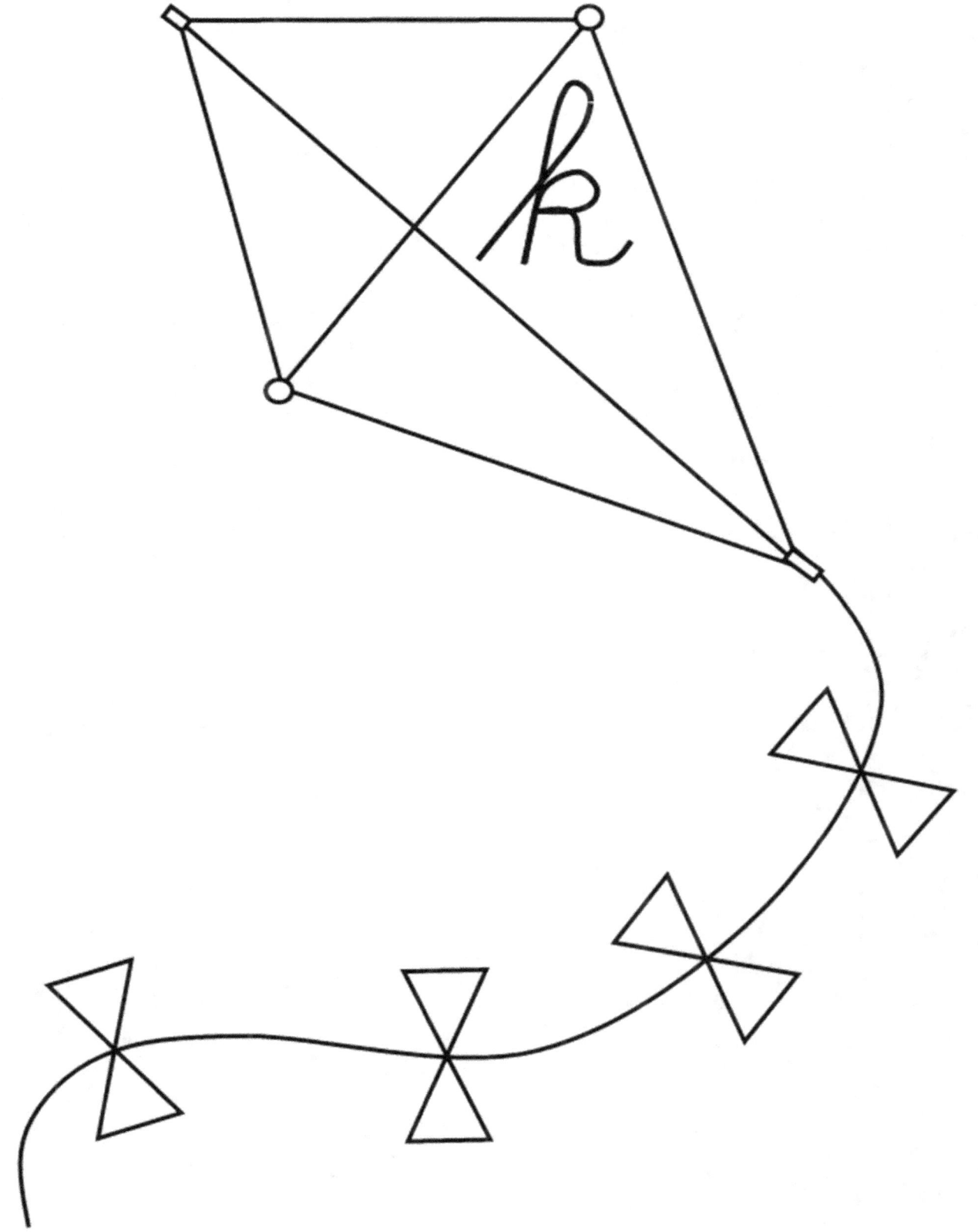

Trace the steps for making the letter k on the following line.

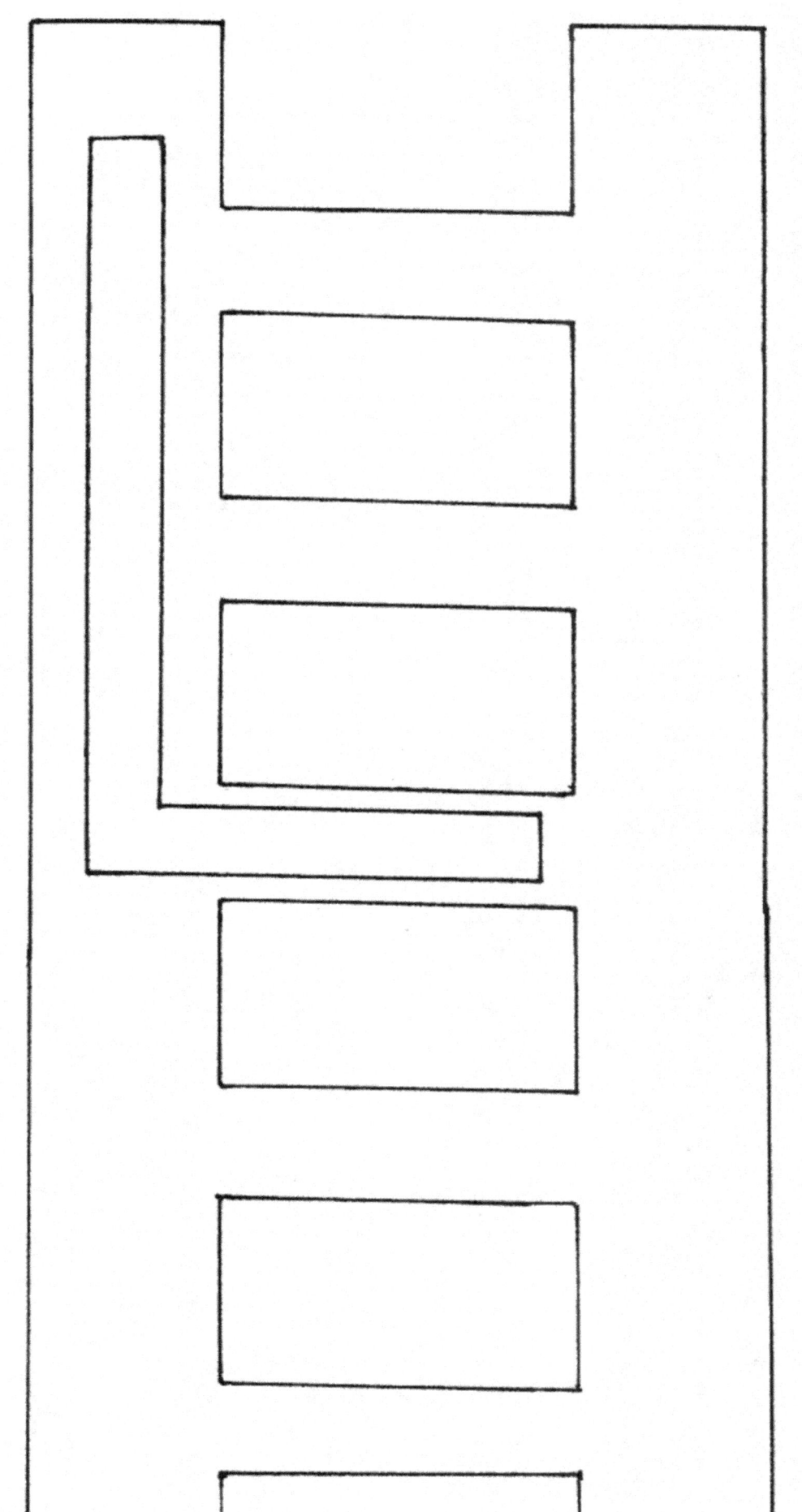

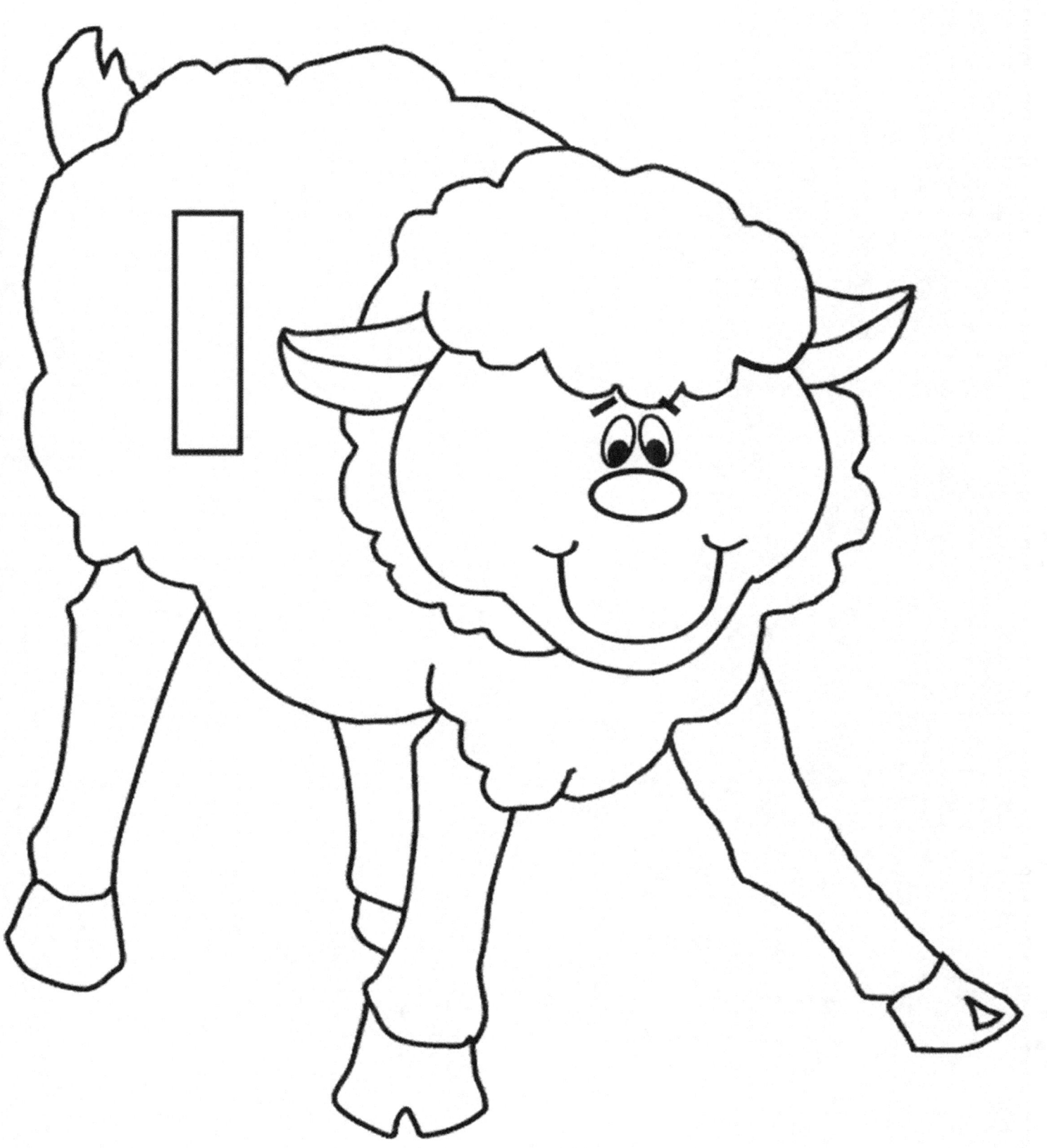

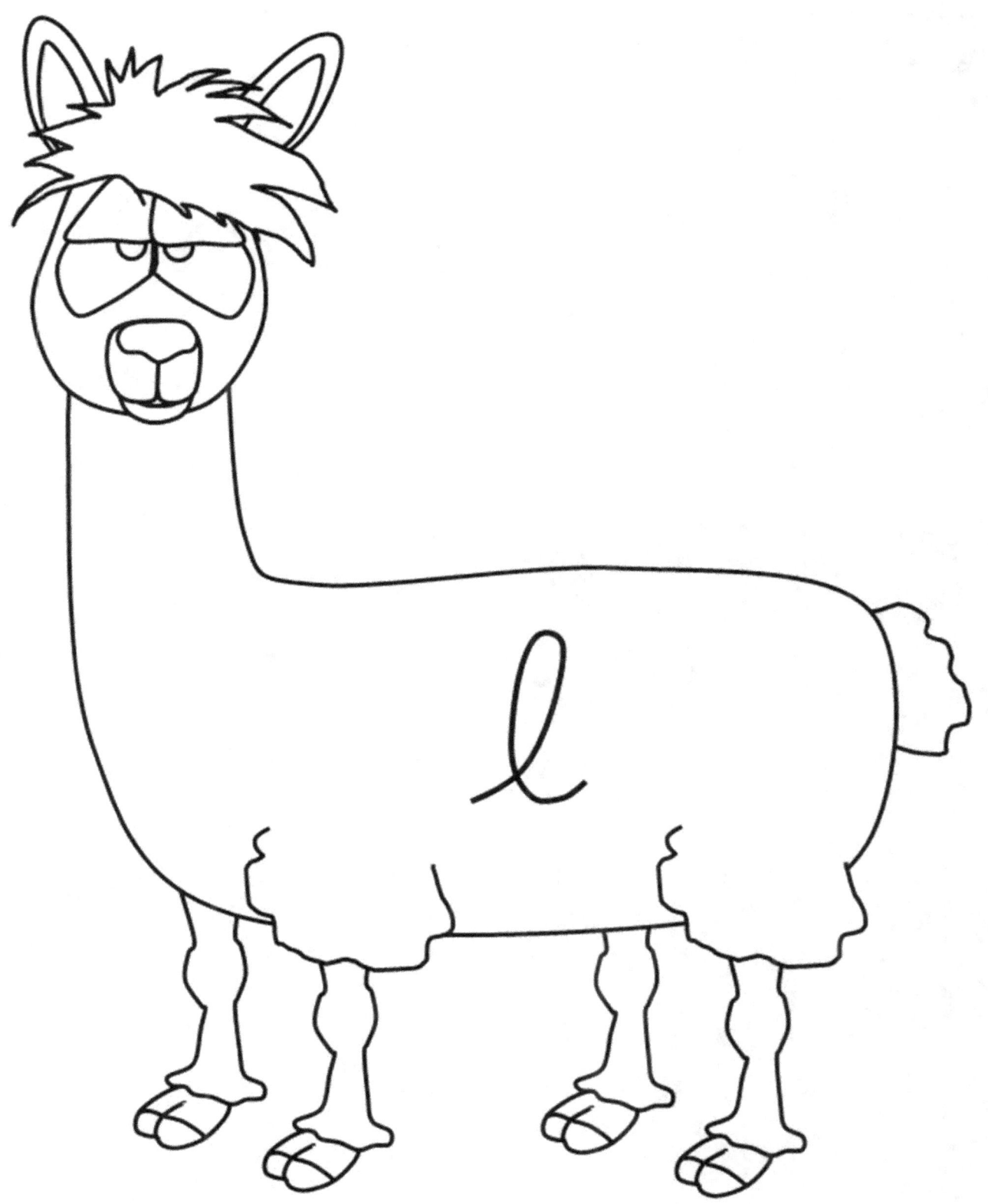

Trace the steps for making the letter l on the following line.

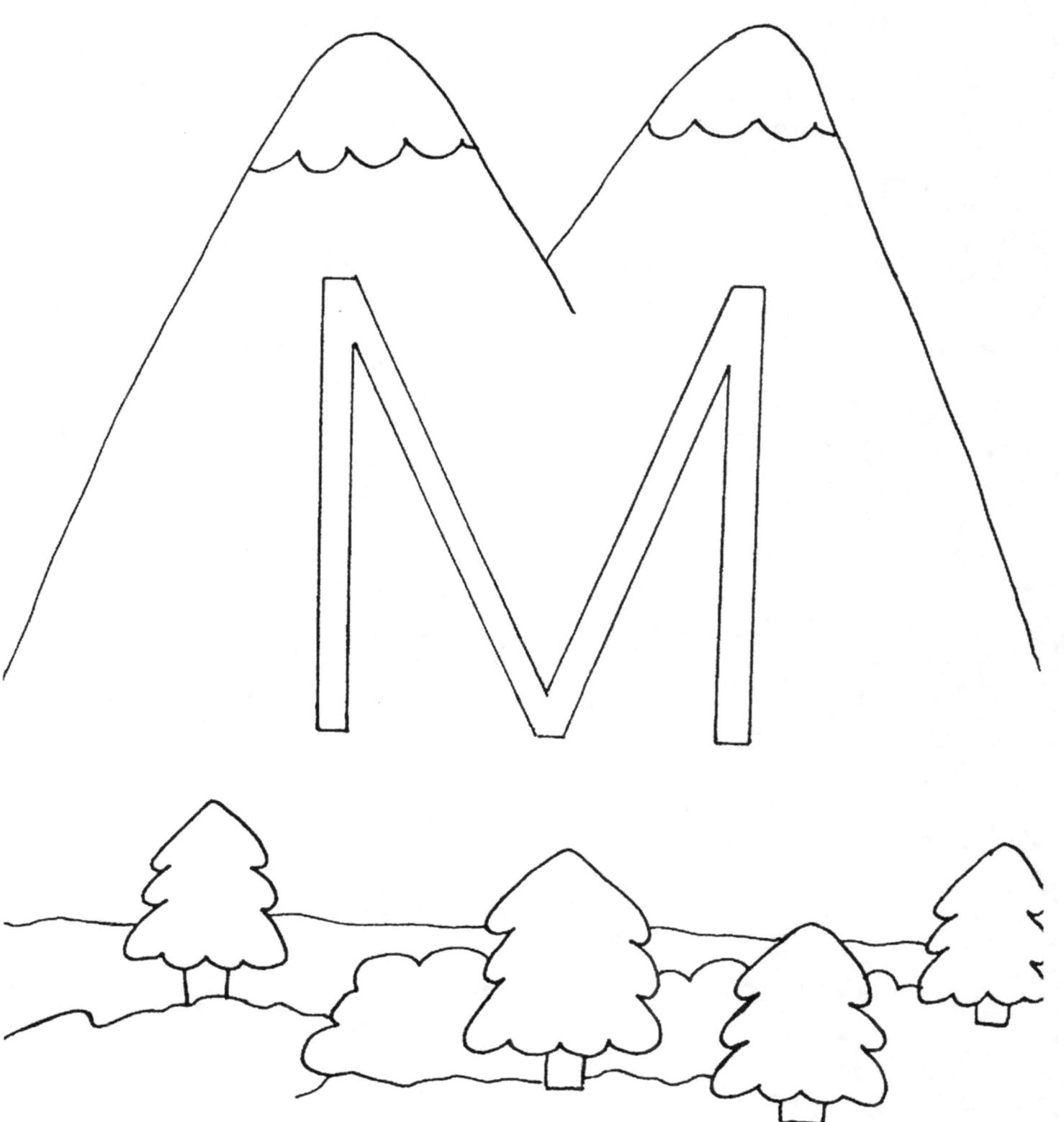

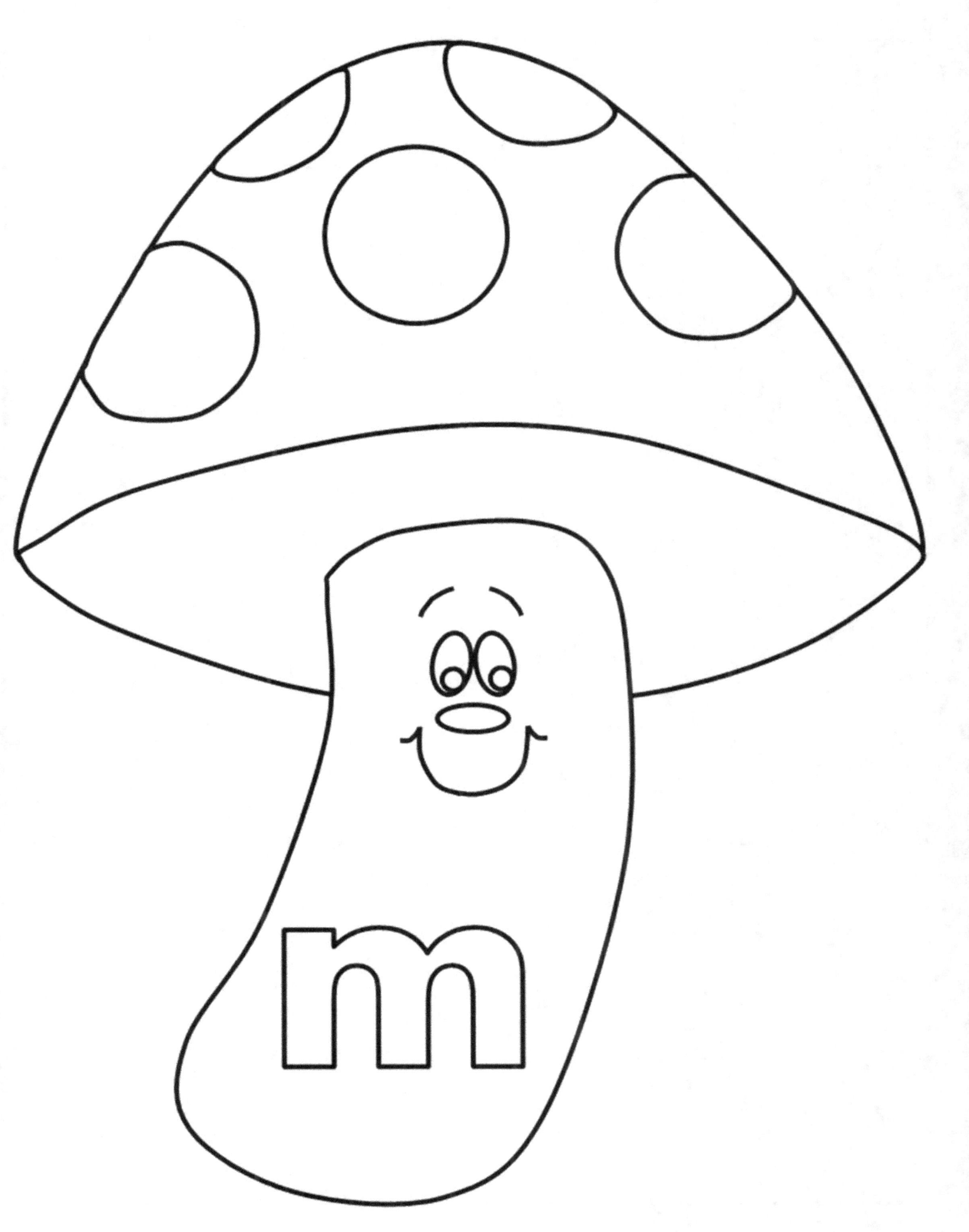

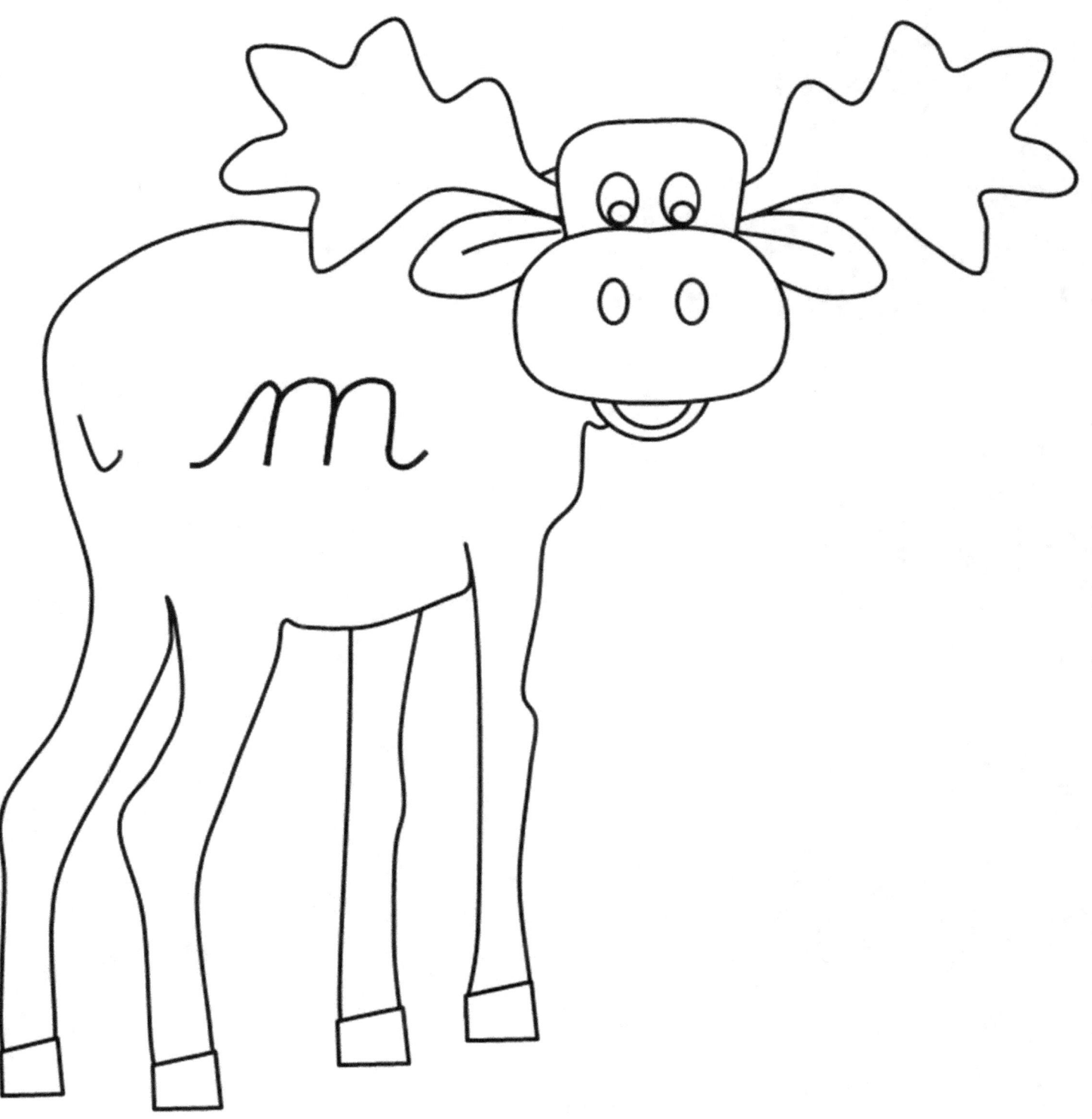

Trace the steps for making the letter m on the following line.

_____

ˌ ˌ ˌ m m m m m m m

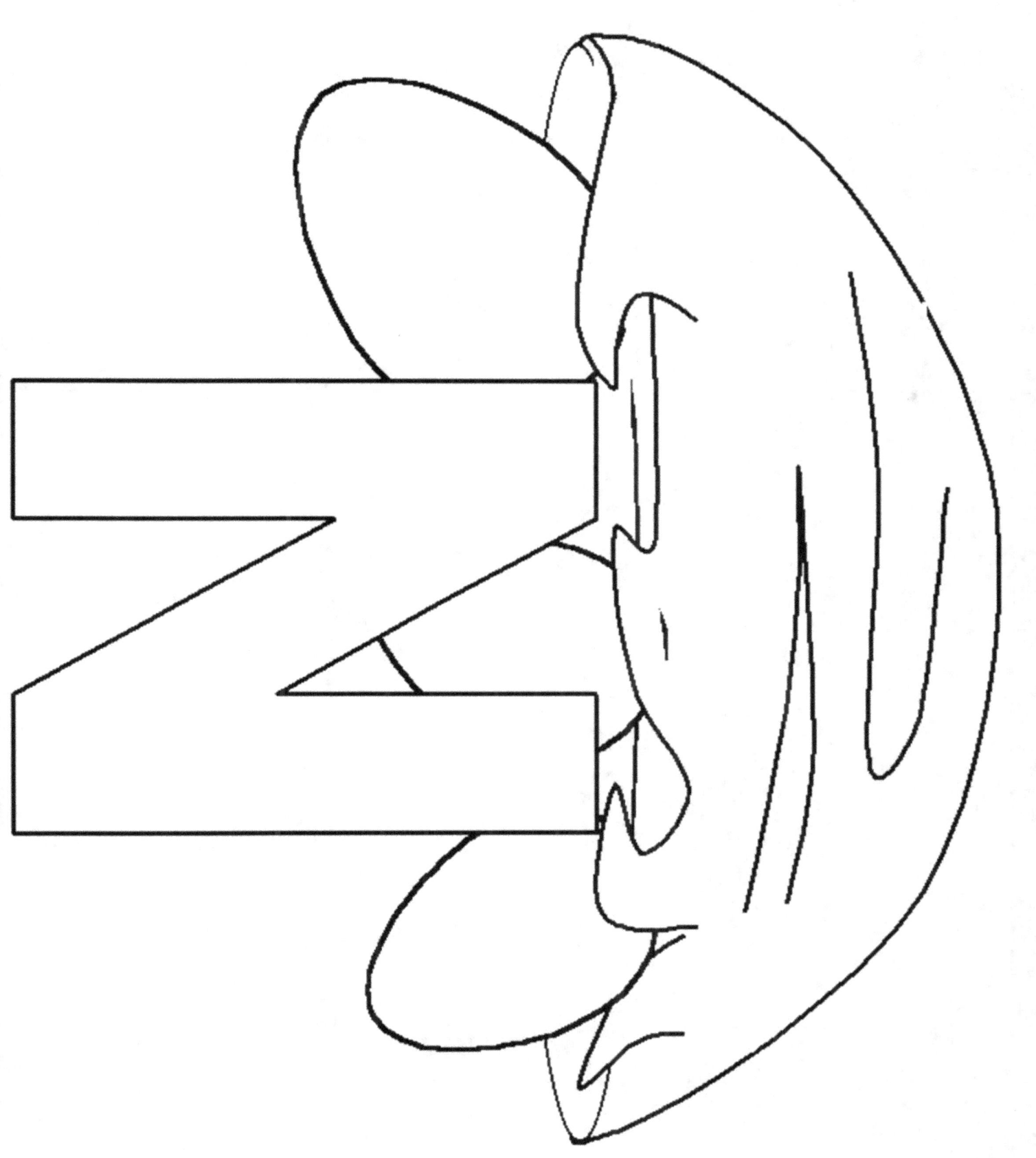

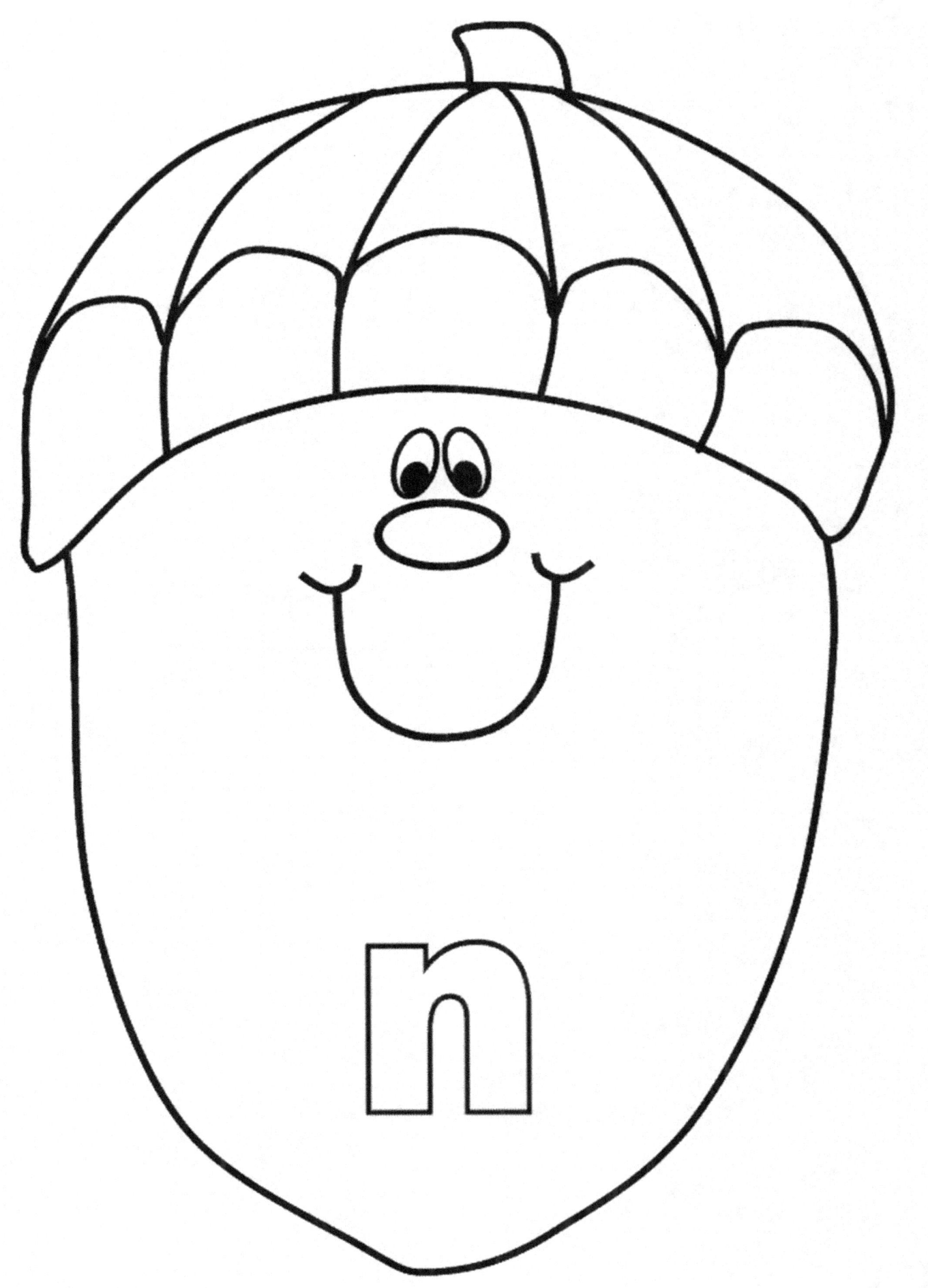

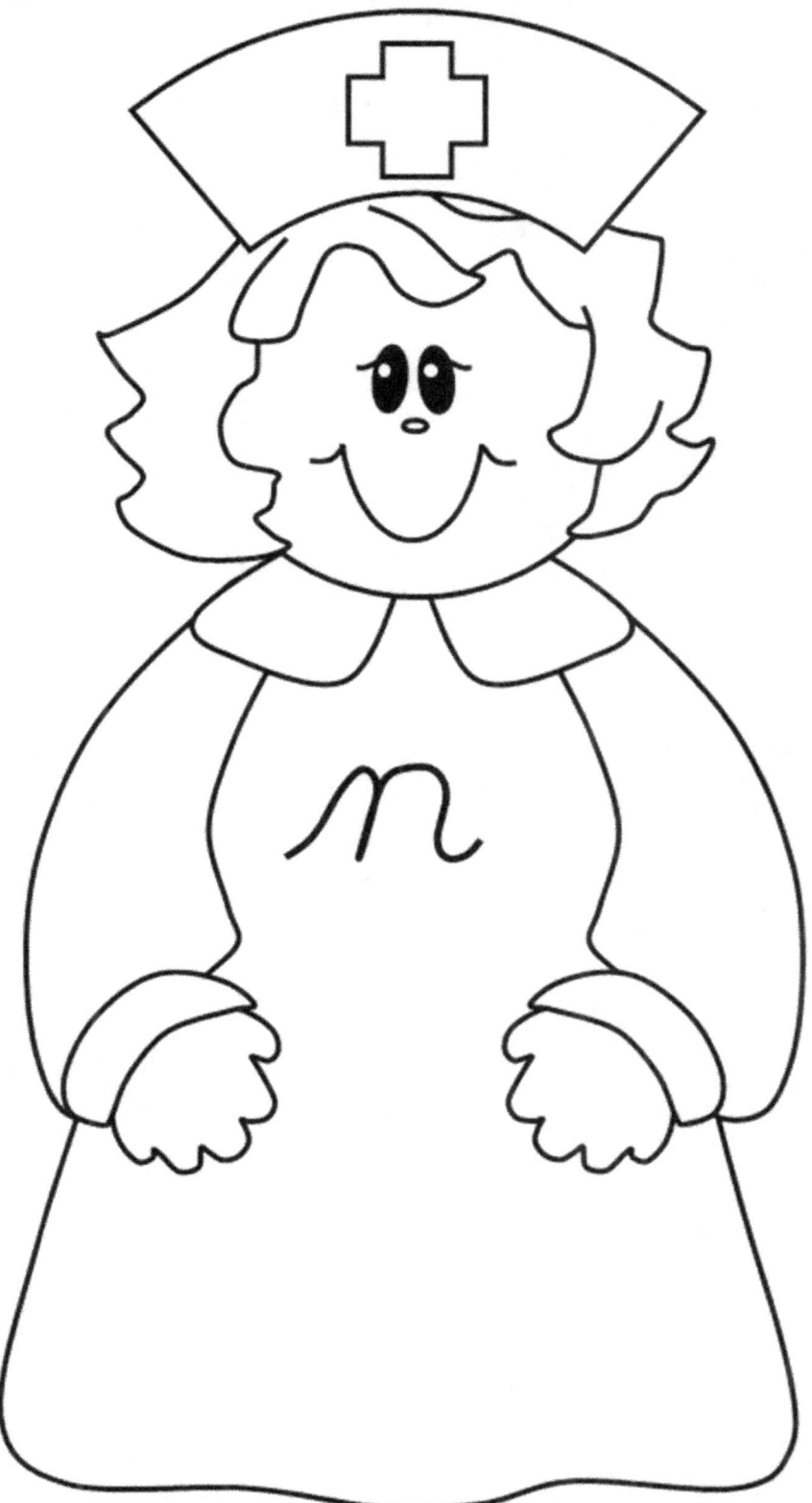

Trace the steps for making the letter n on the following line.

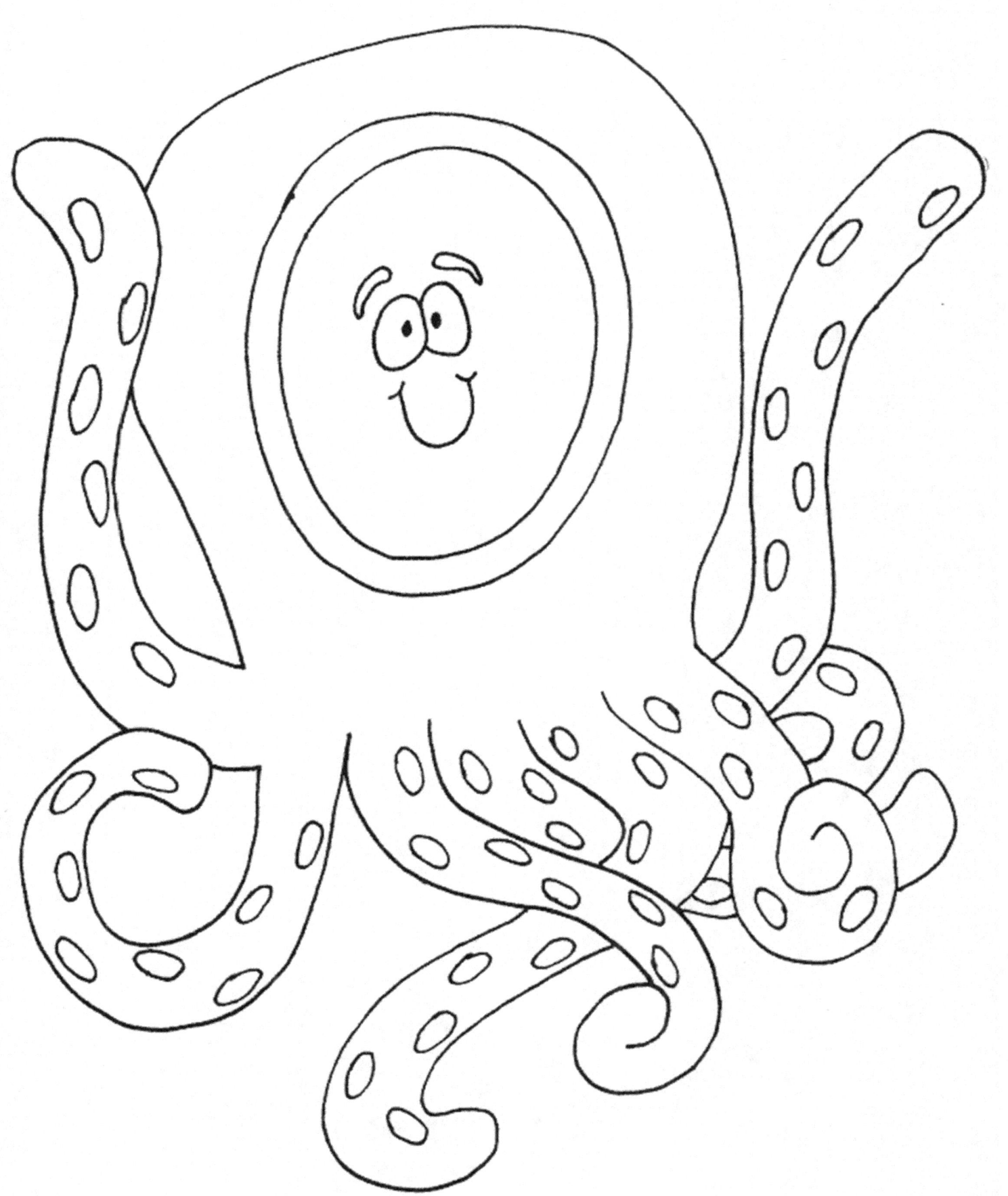

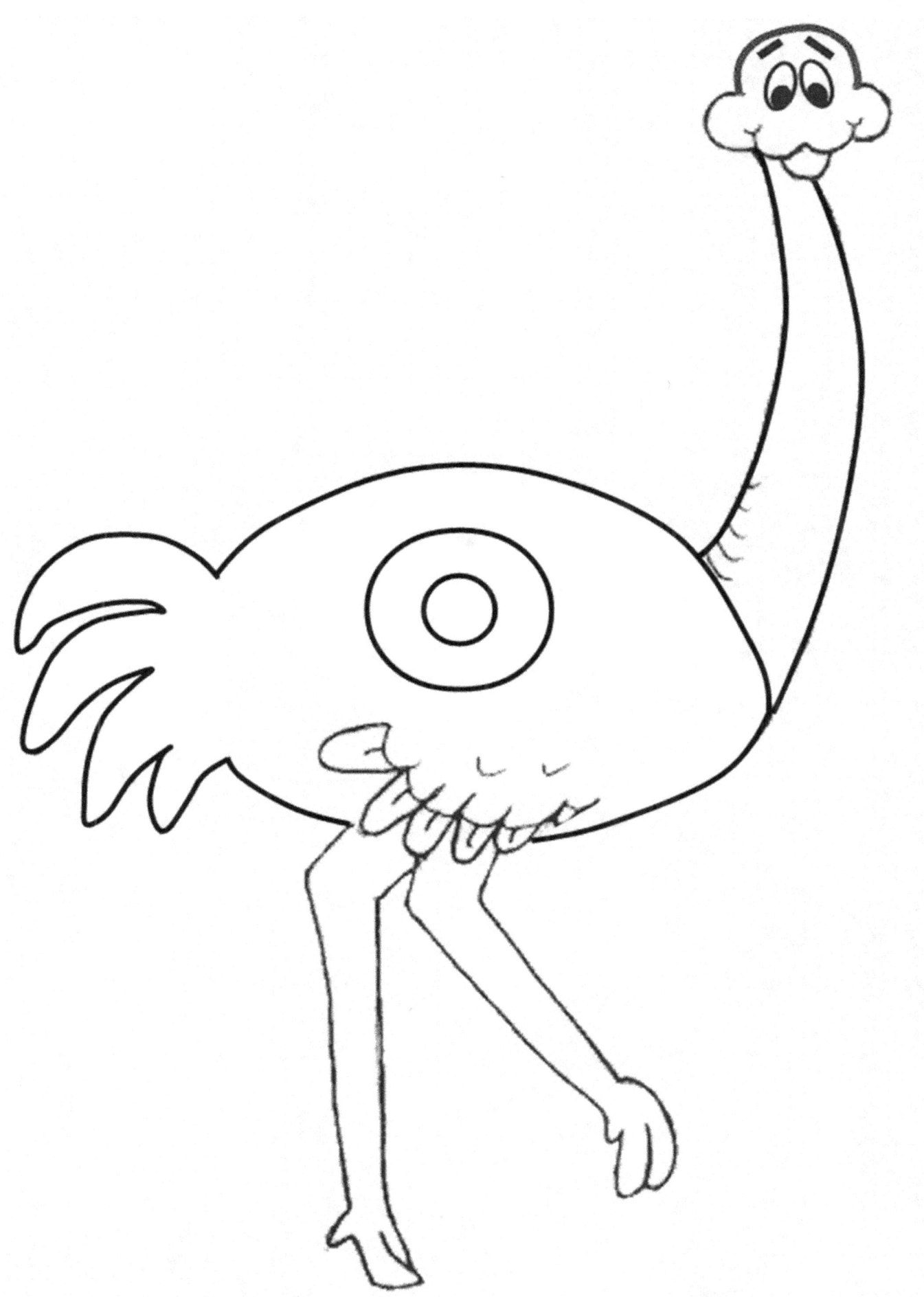

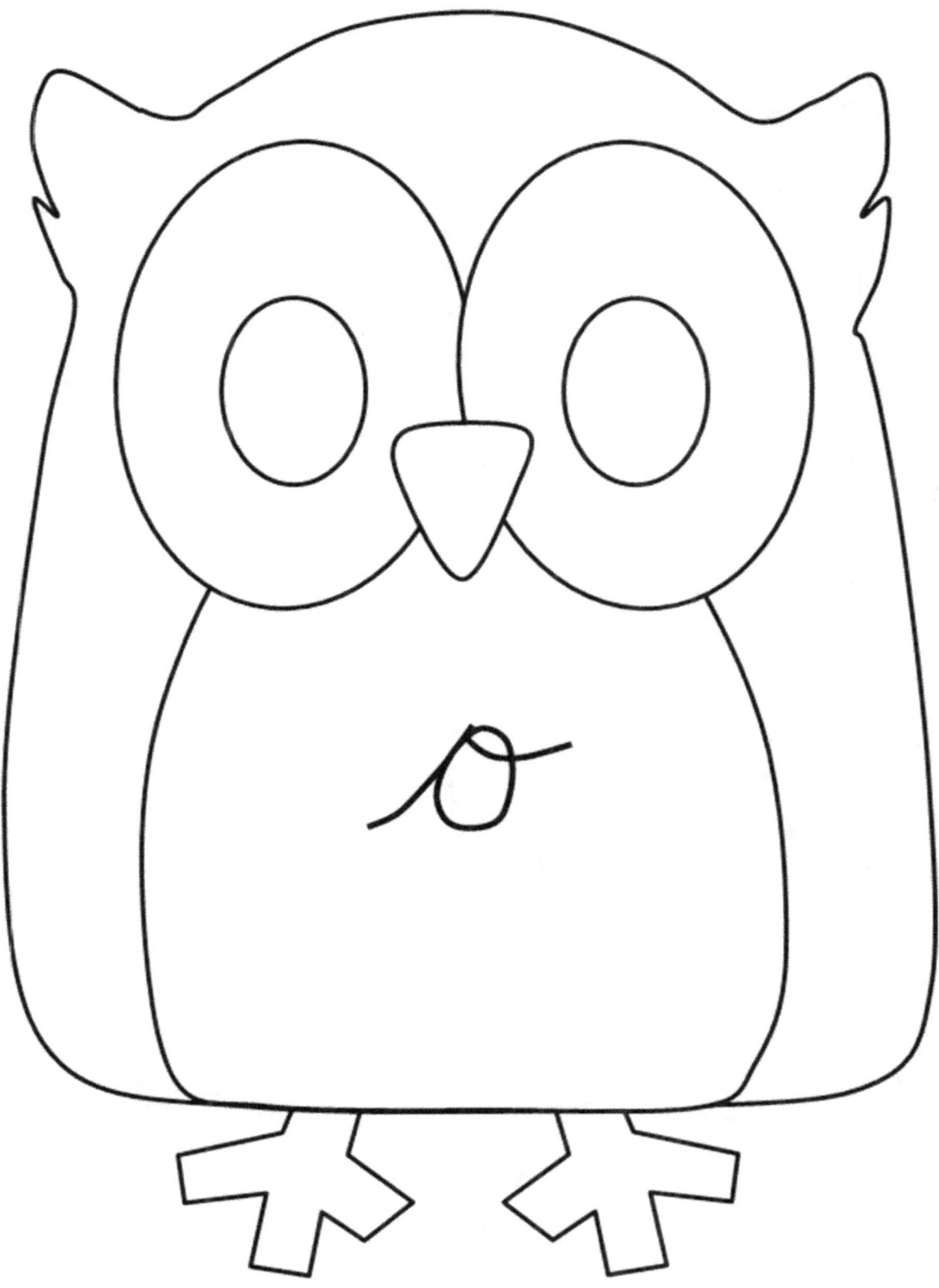

Trace the steps for making the letter o on the following line.

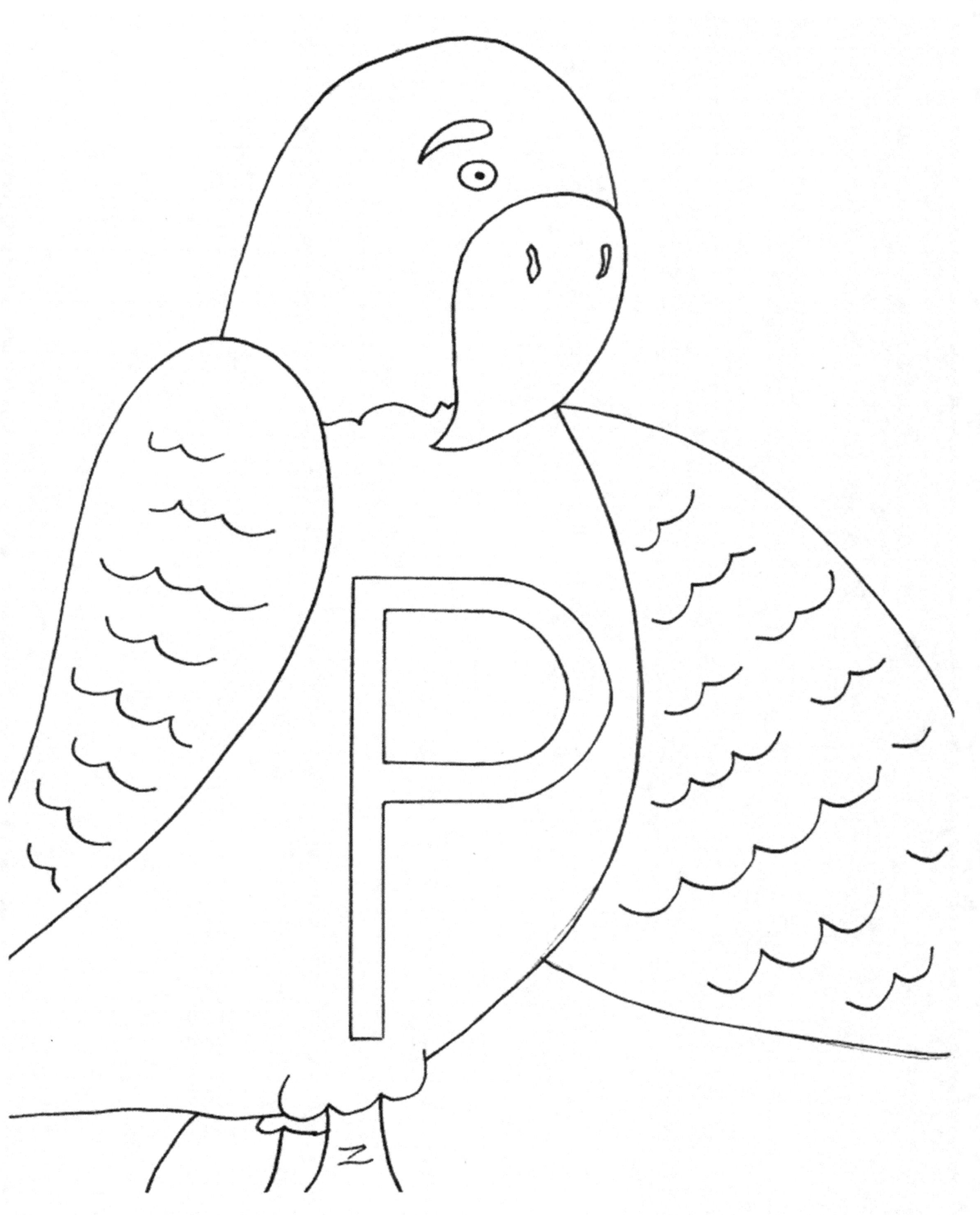

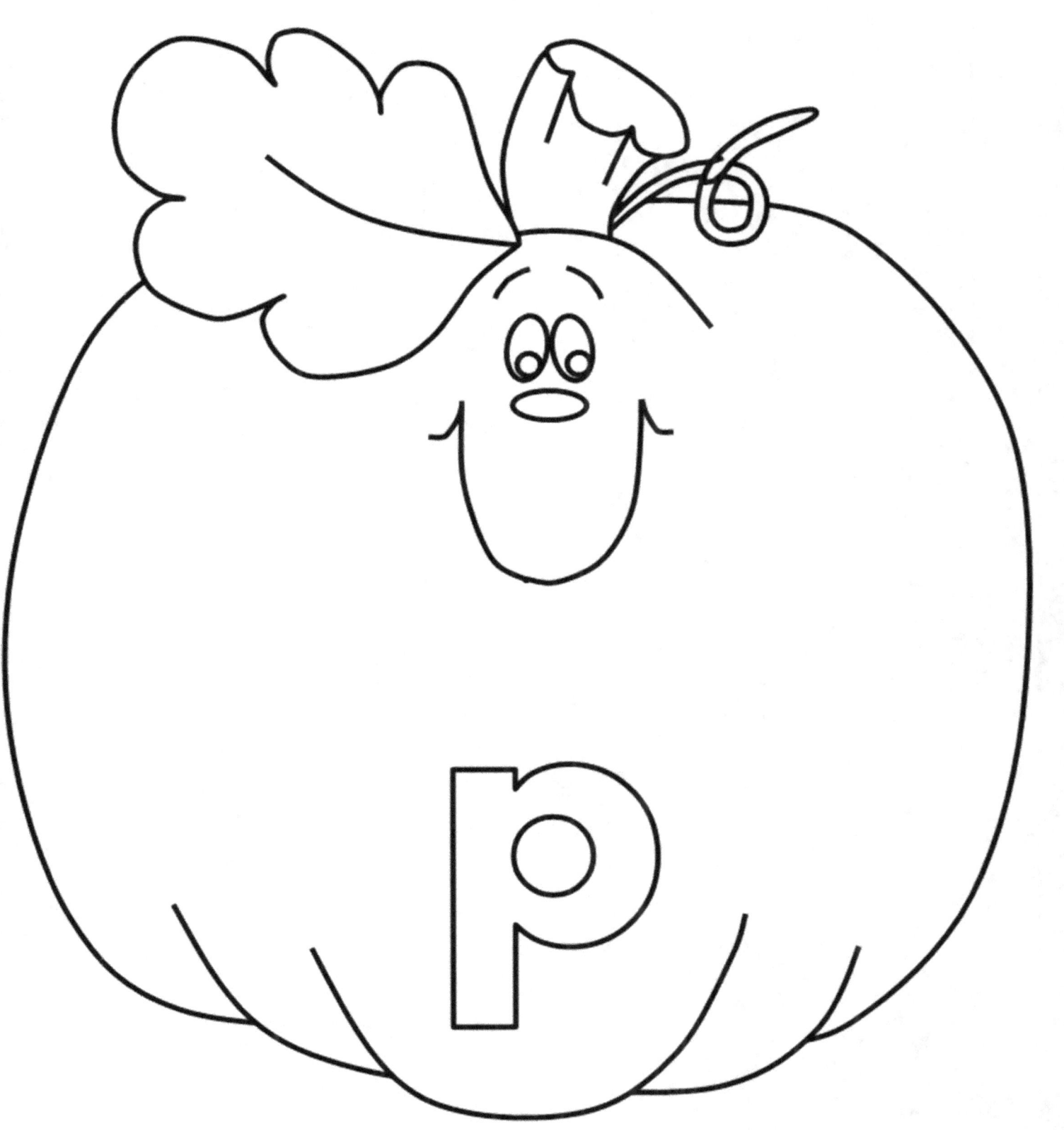

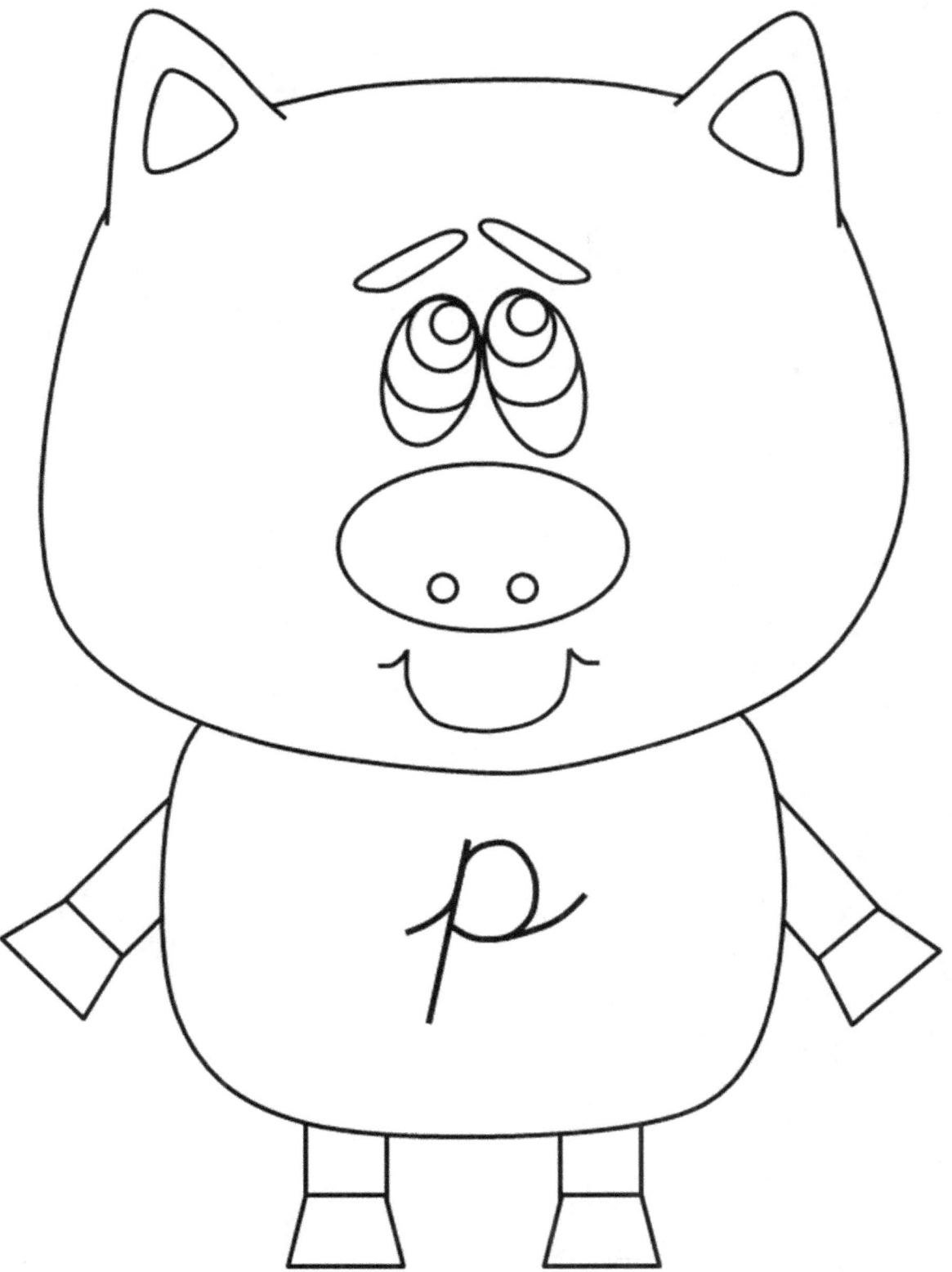

Trace the steps for making the letter p on the following line.

_p_ _p_ _p_ _p_ _p_ _pp_

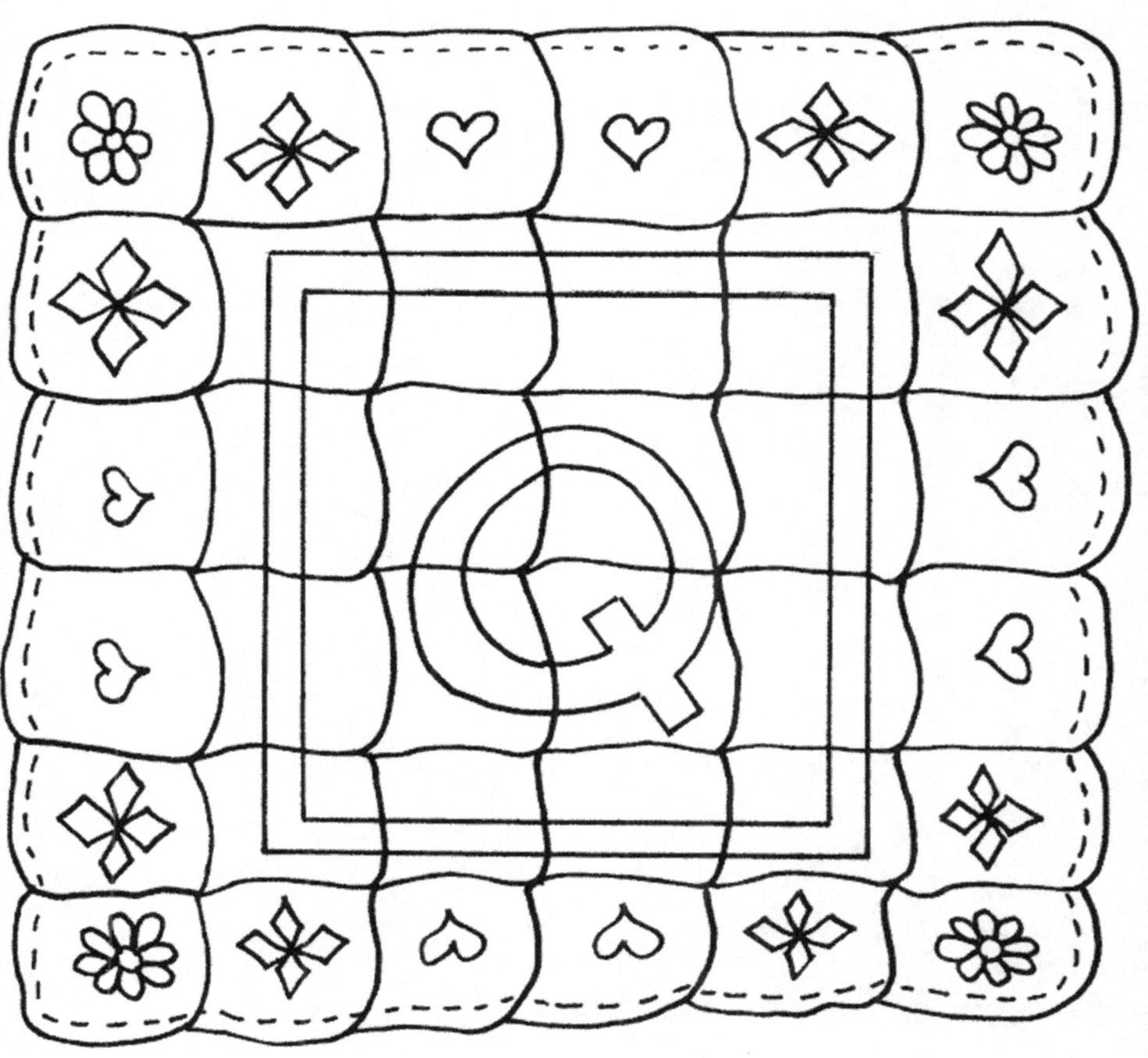

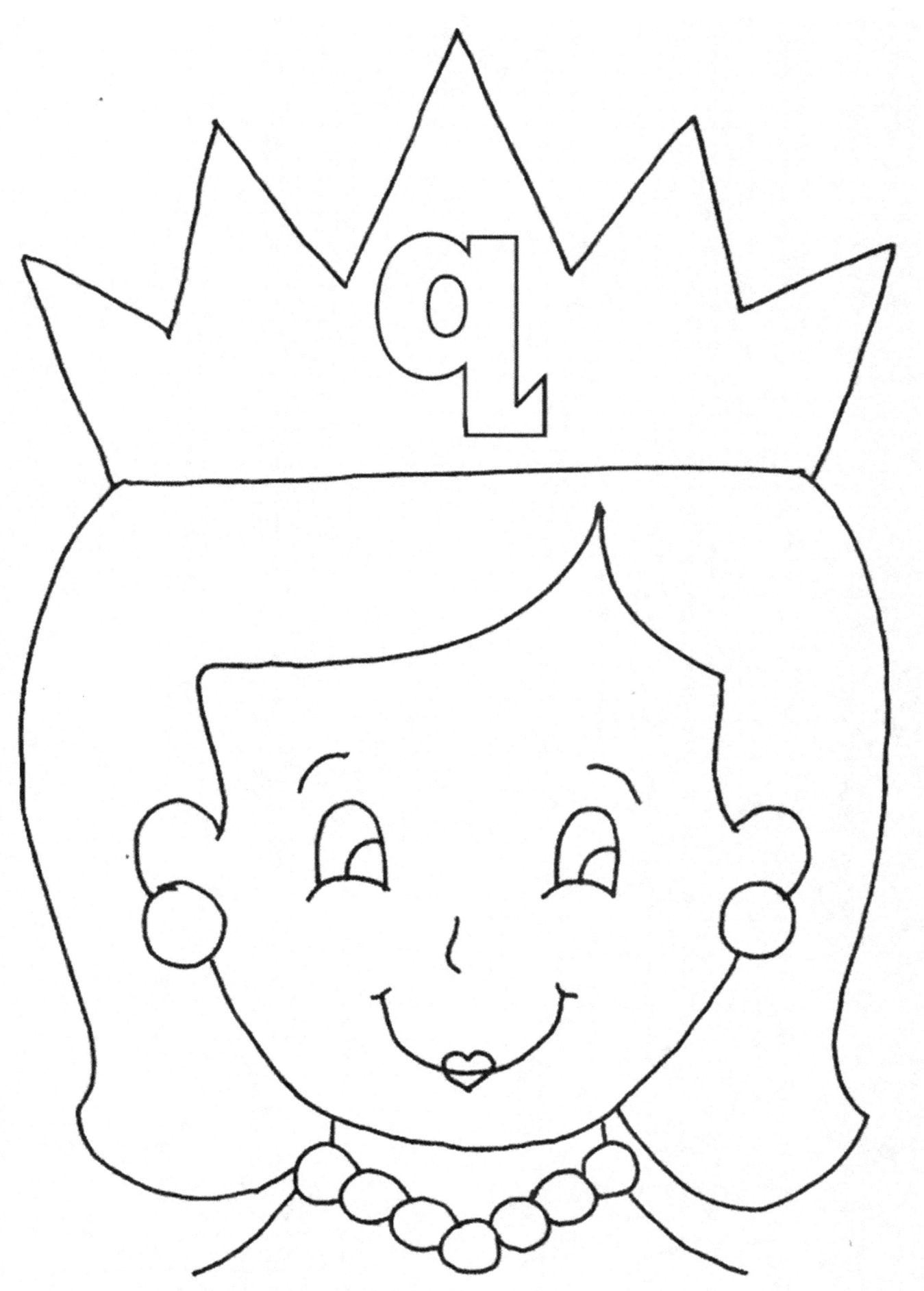

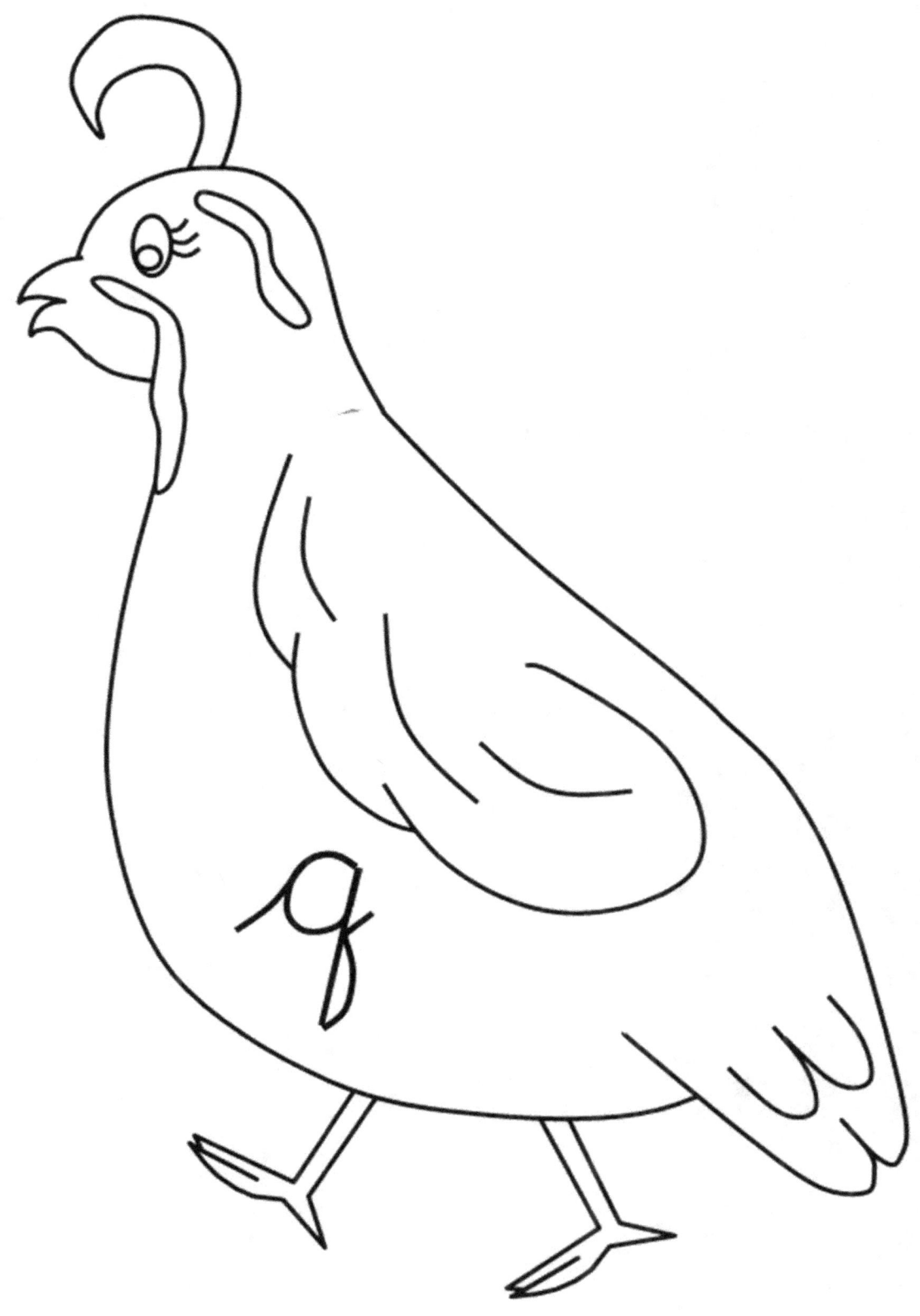

Trace the steps for making the letter q on the following line.

_____

r   c   o   q   q   q   q

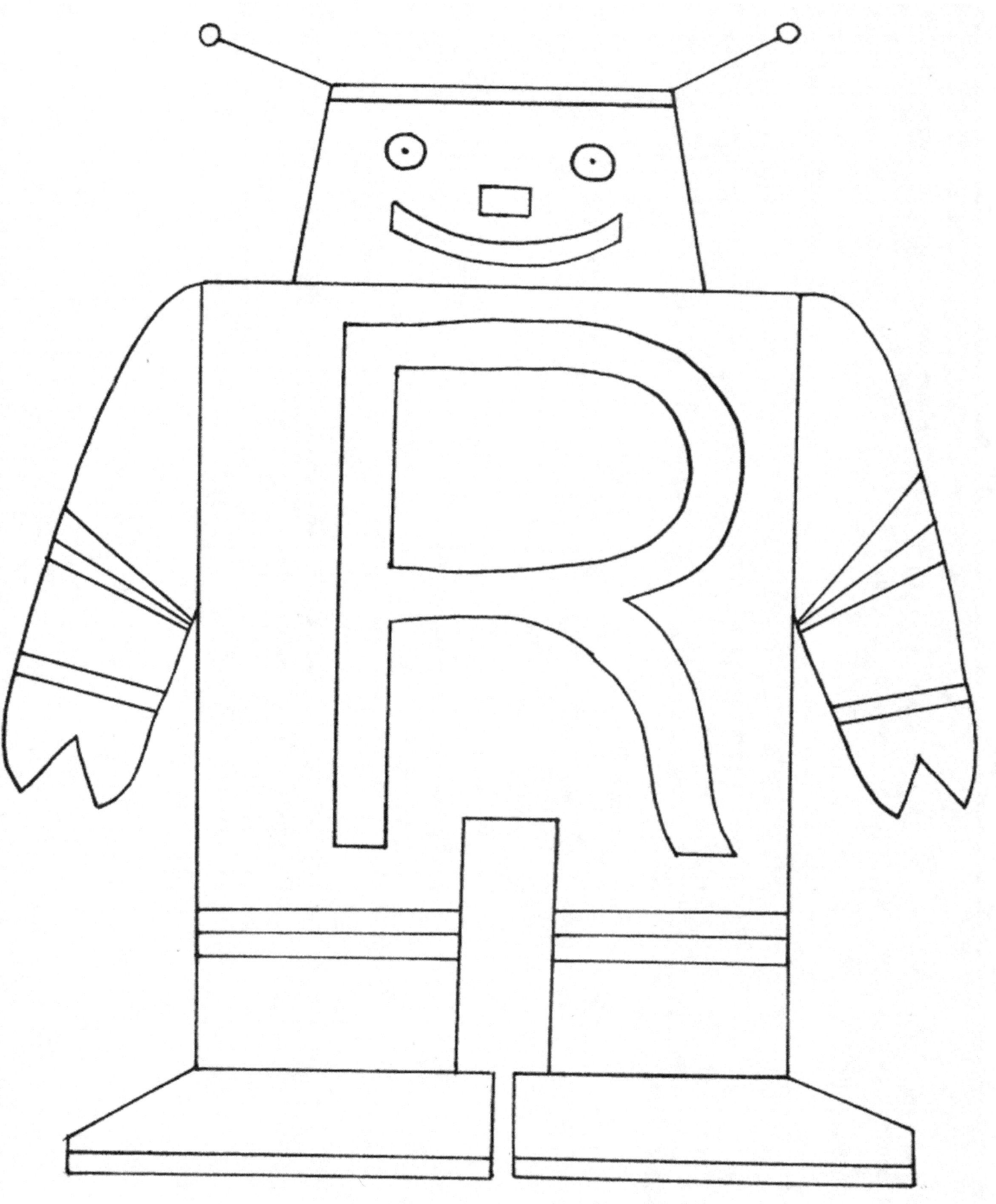

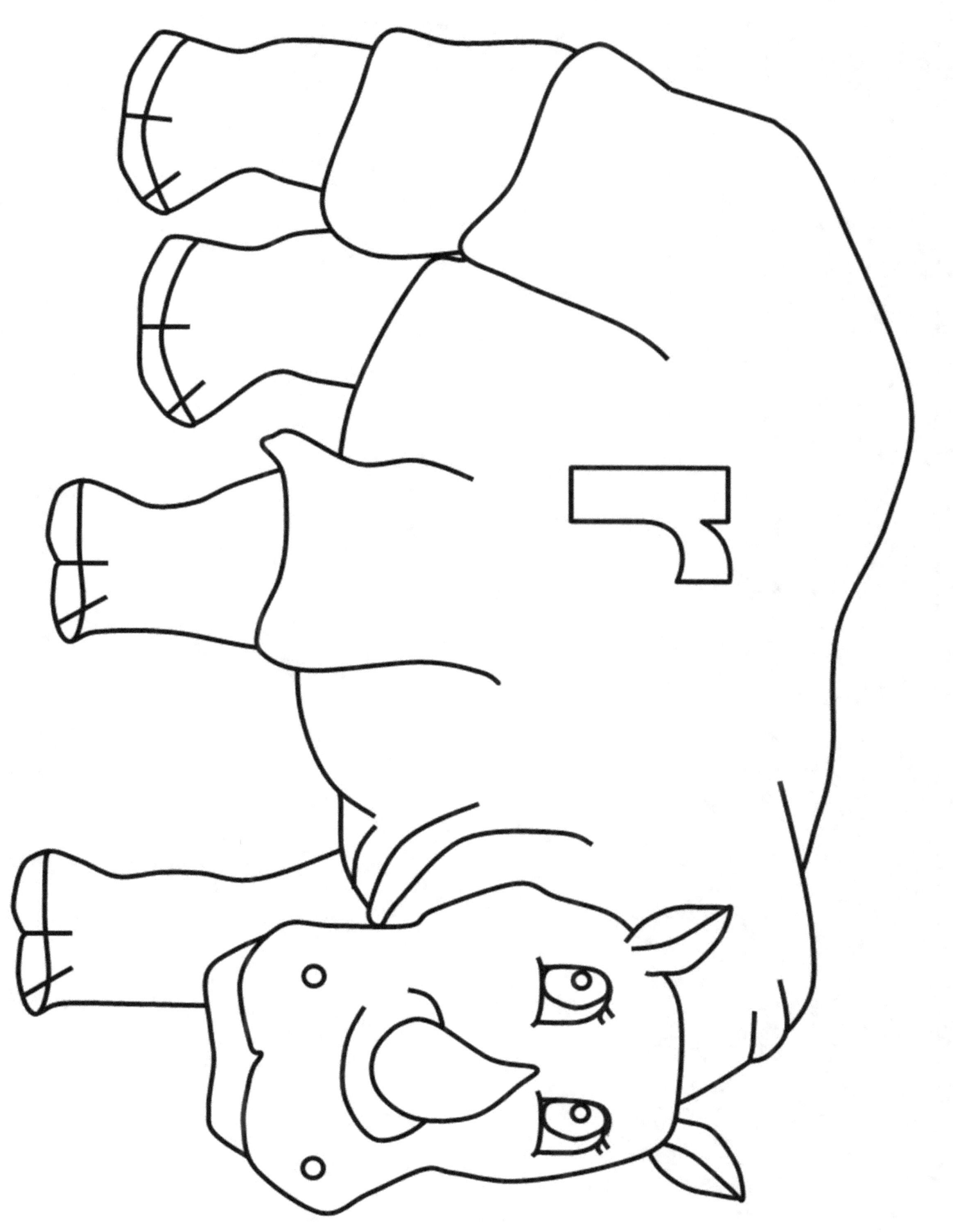

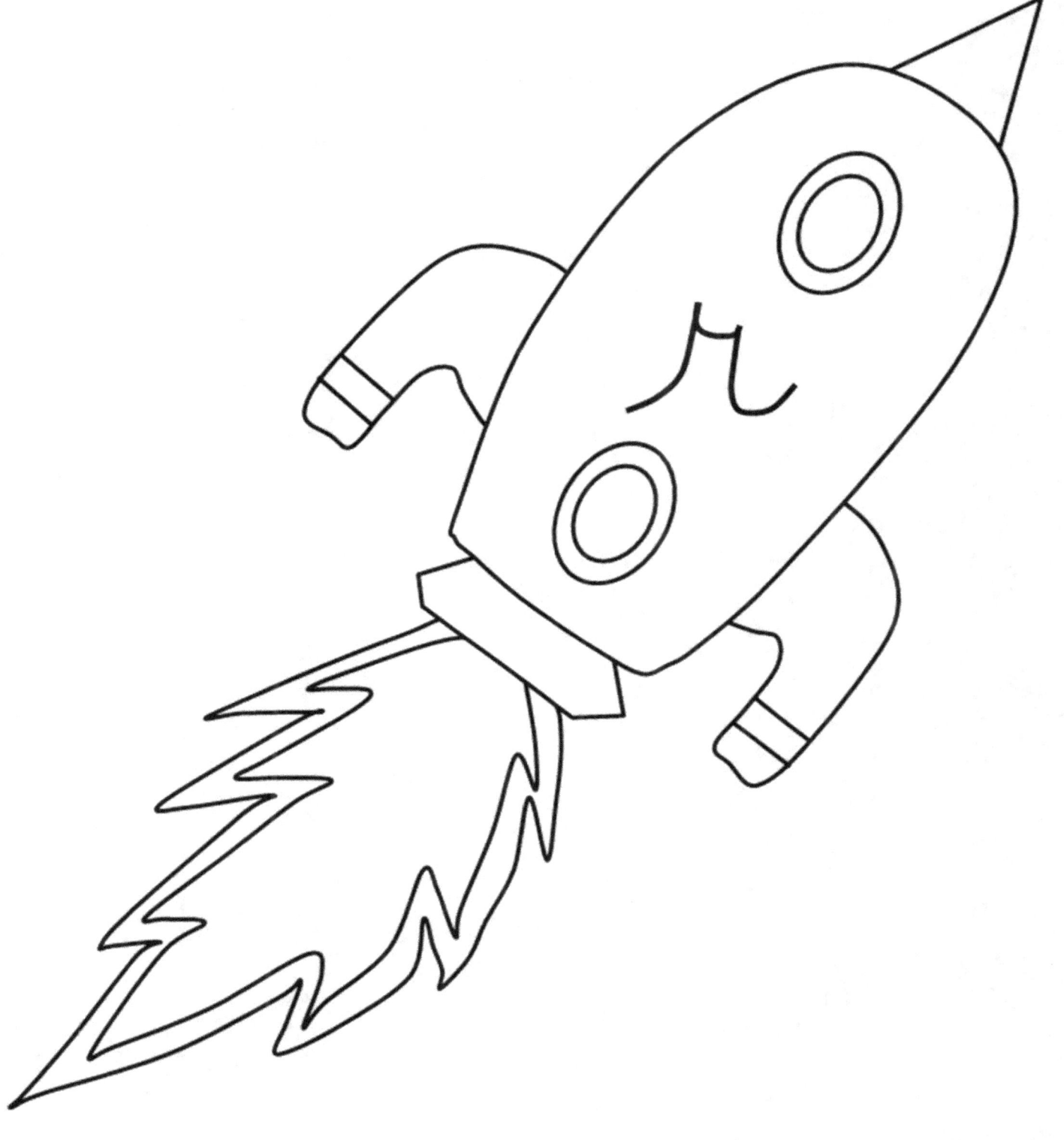

Trace the steps for making the letter r on the following line.

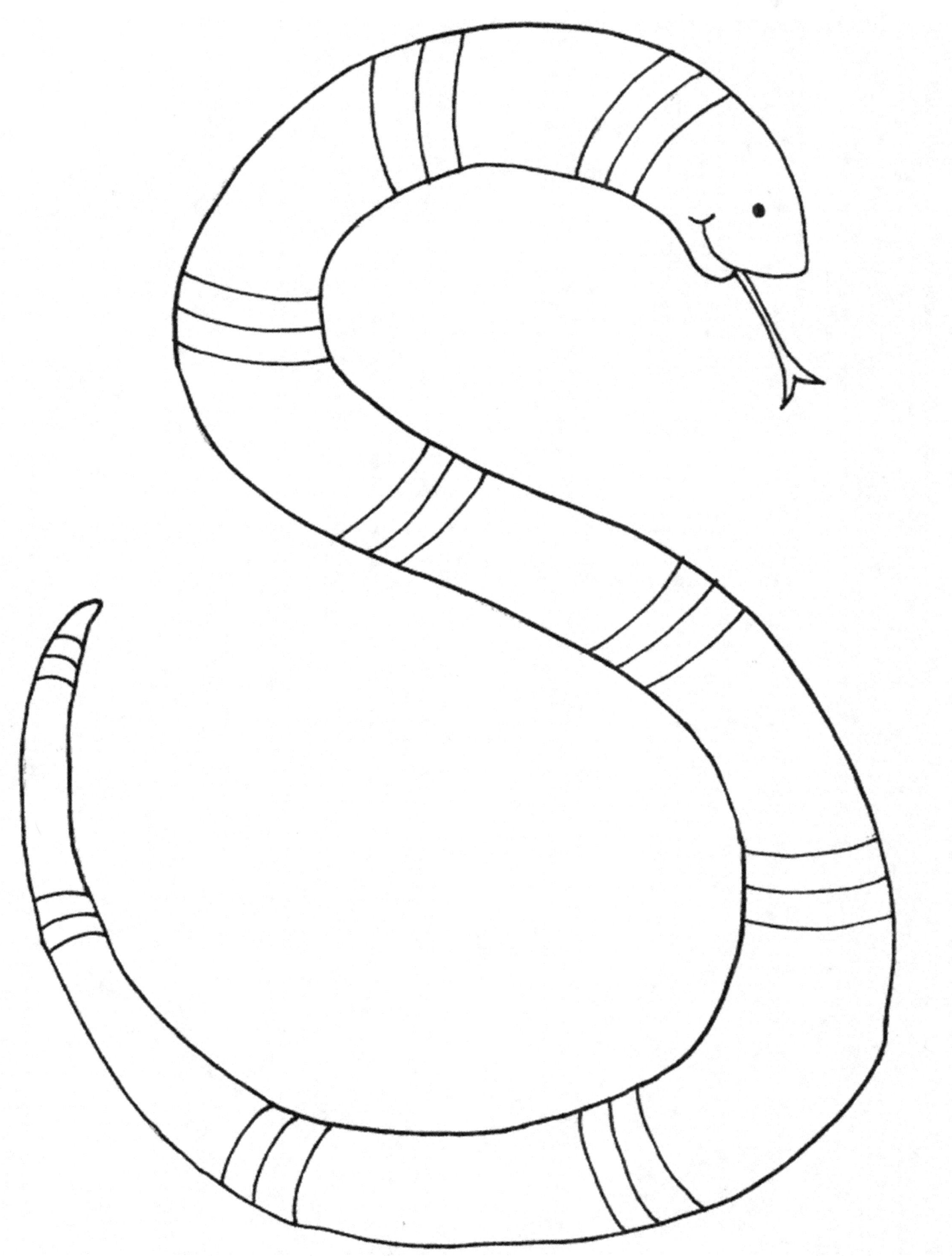

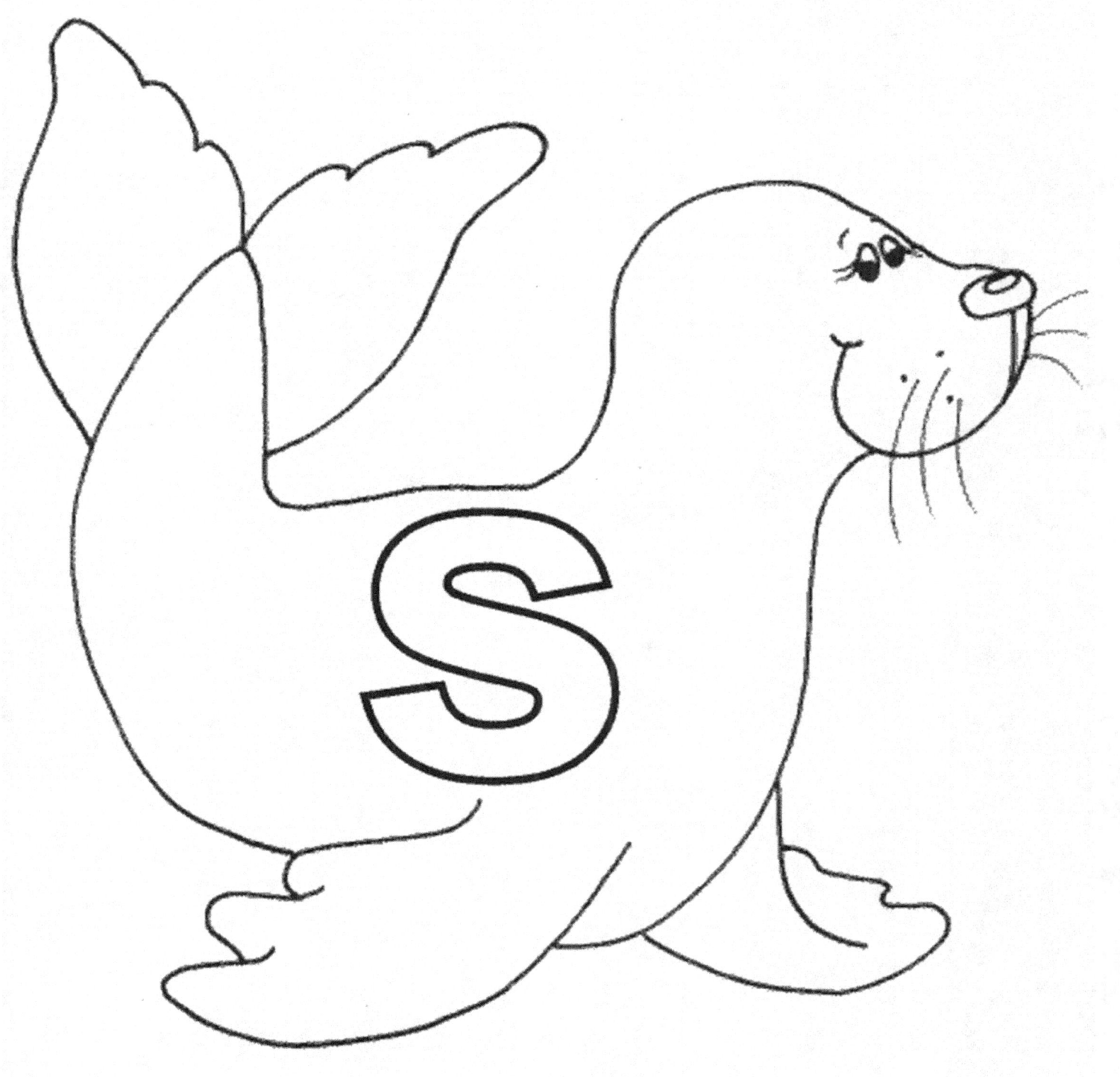

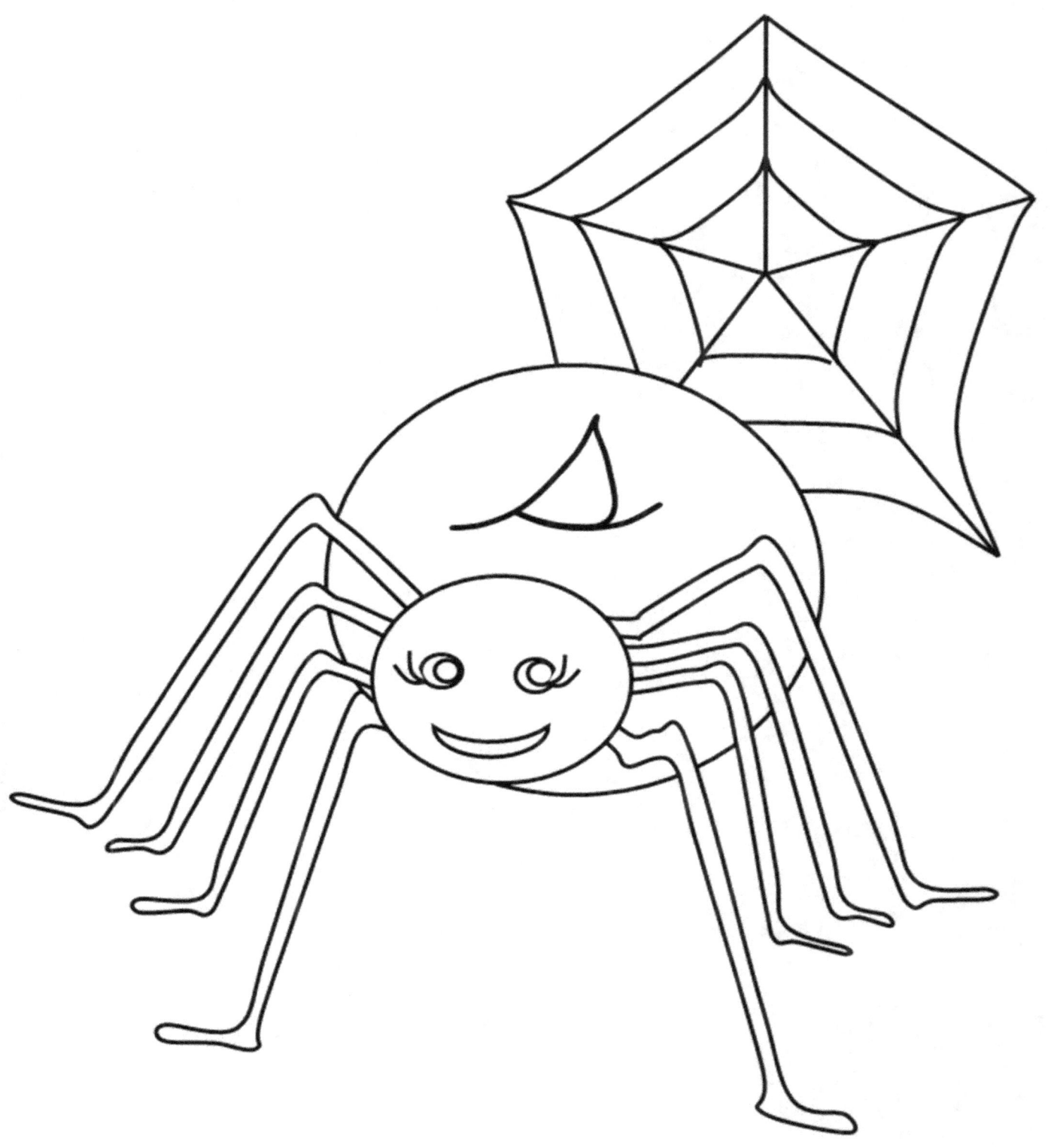

Trace the steps for making the letter s on the following line.

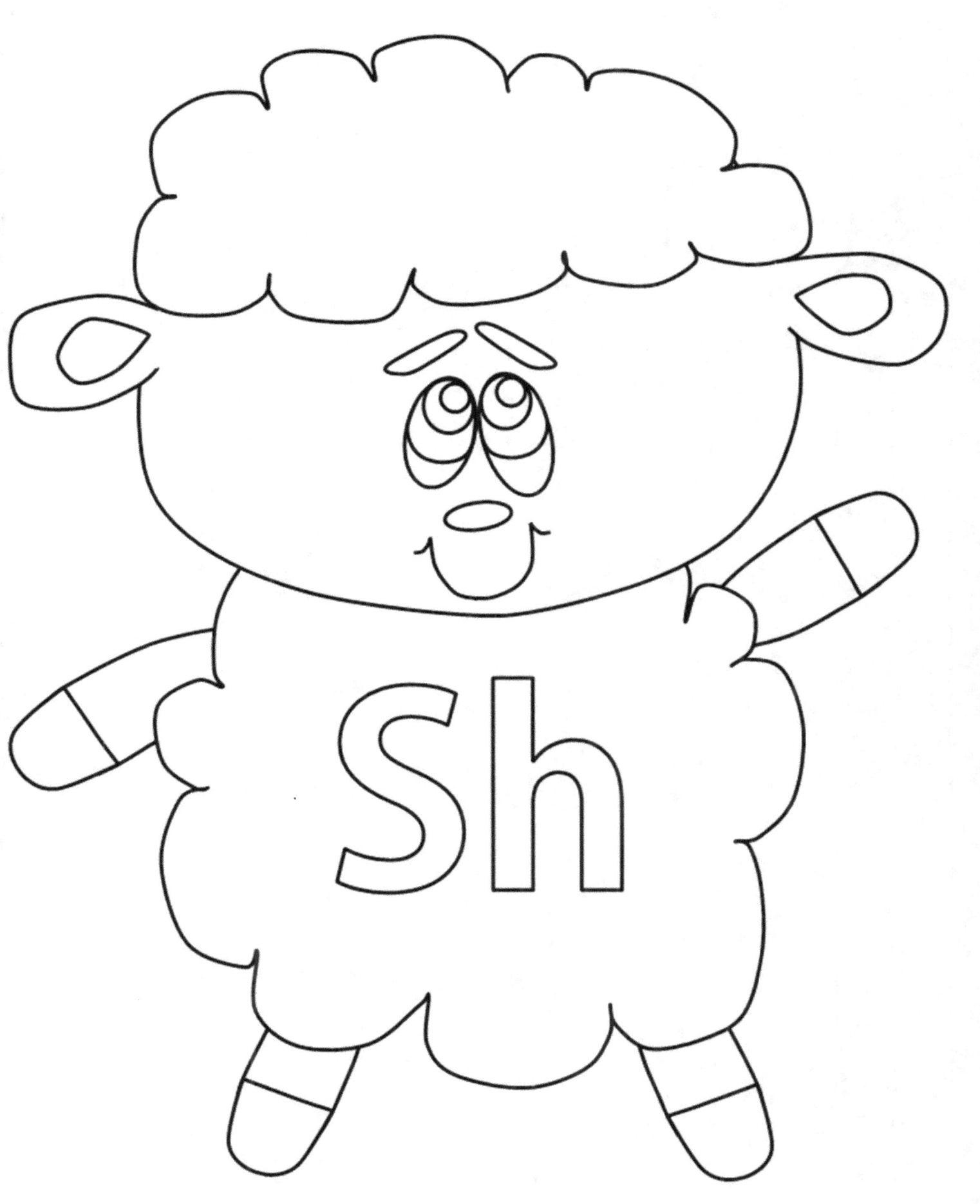

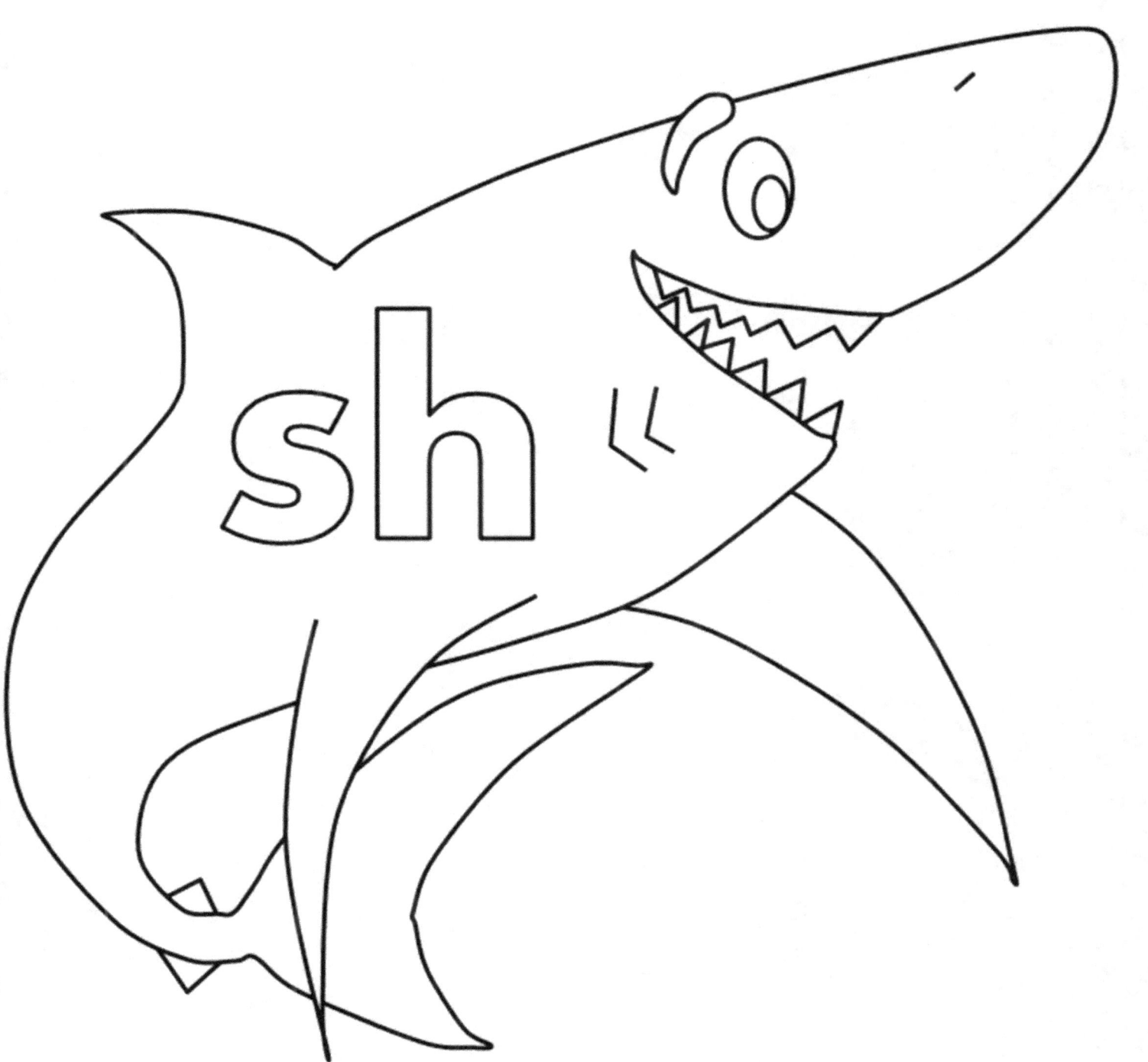

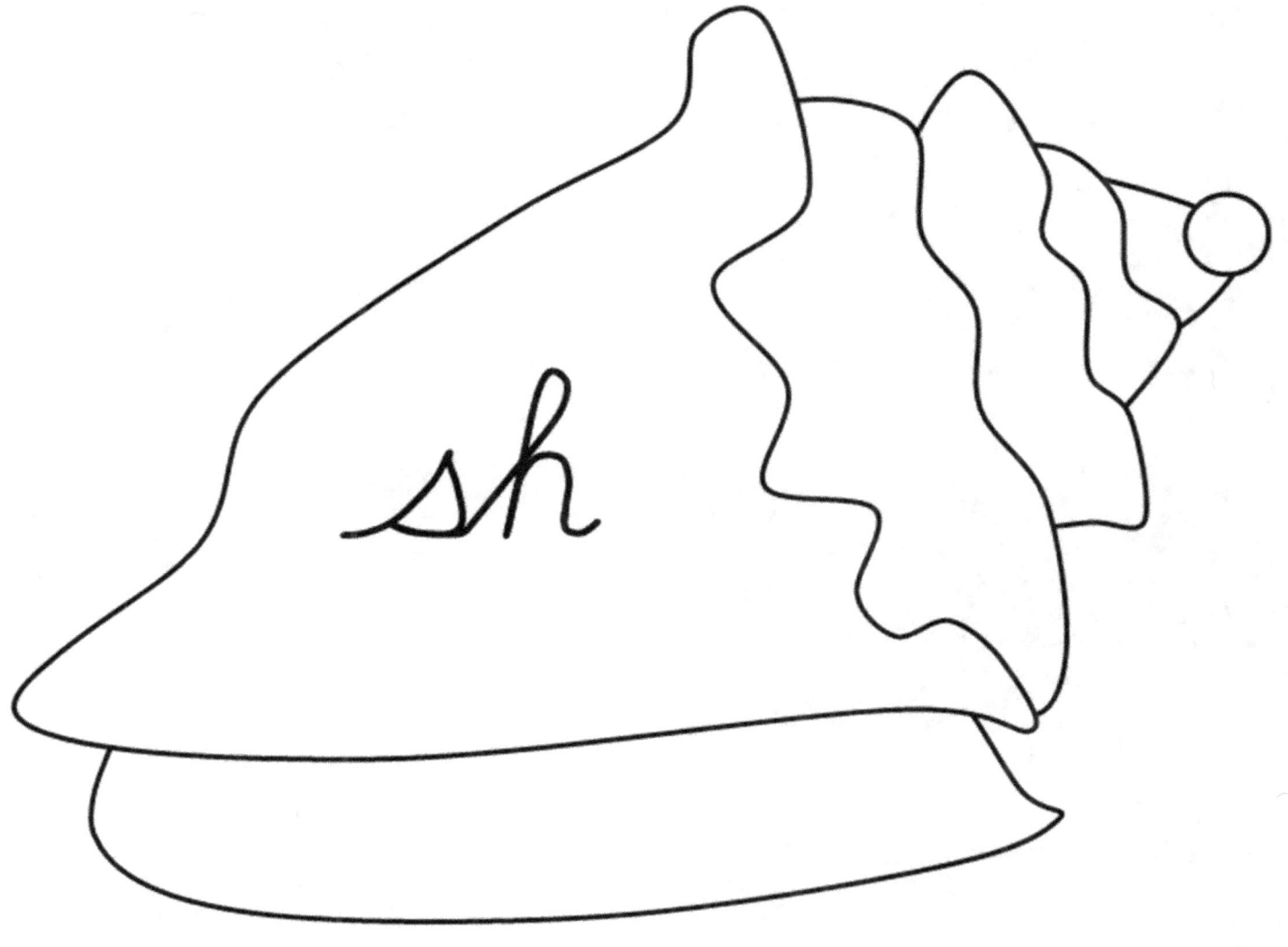

Trace the steps for making the letter sh on the following line.

_s_ _h_ _sh_ _sh_ _sh_ _sh_

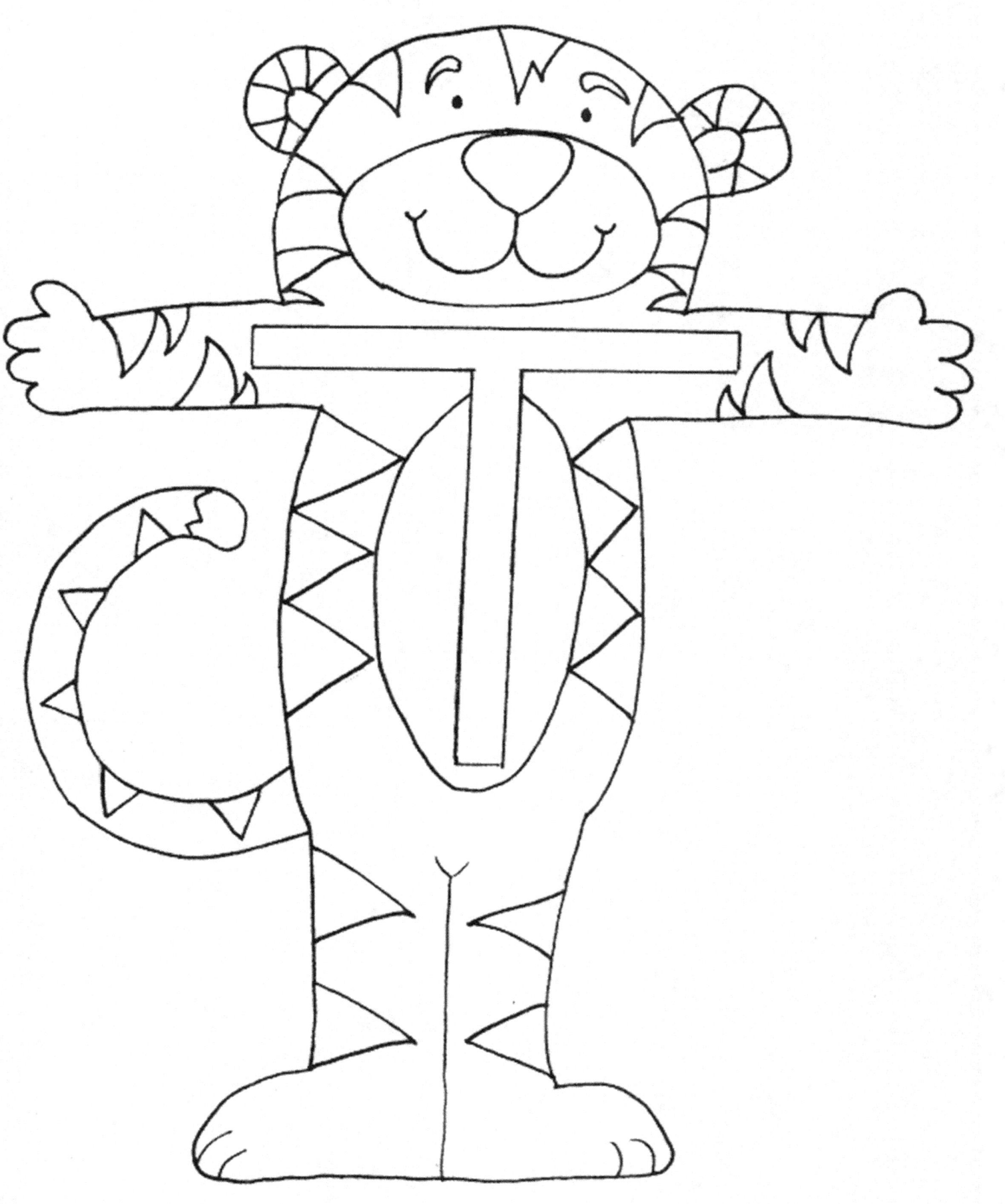

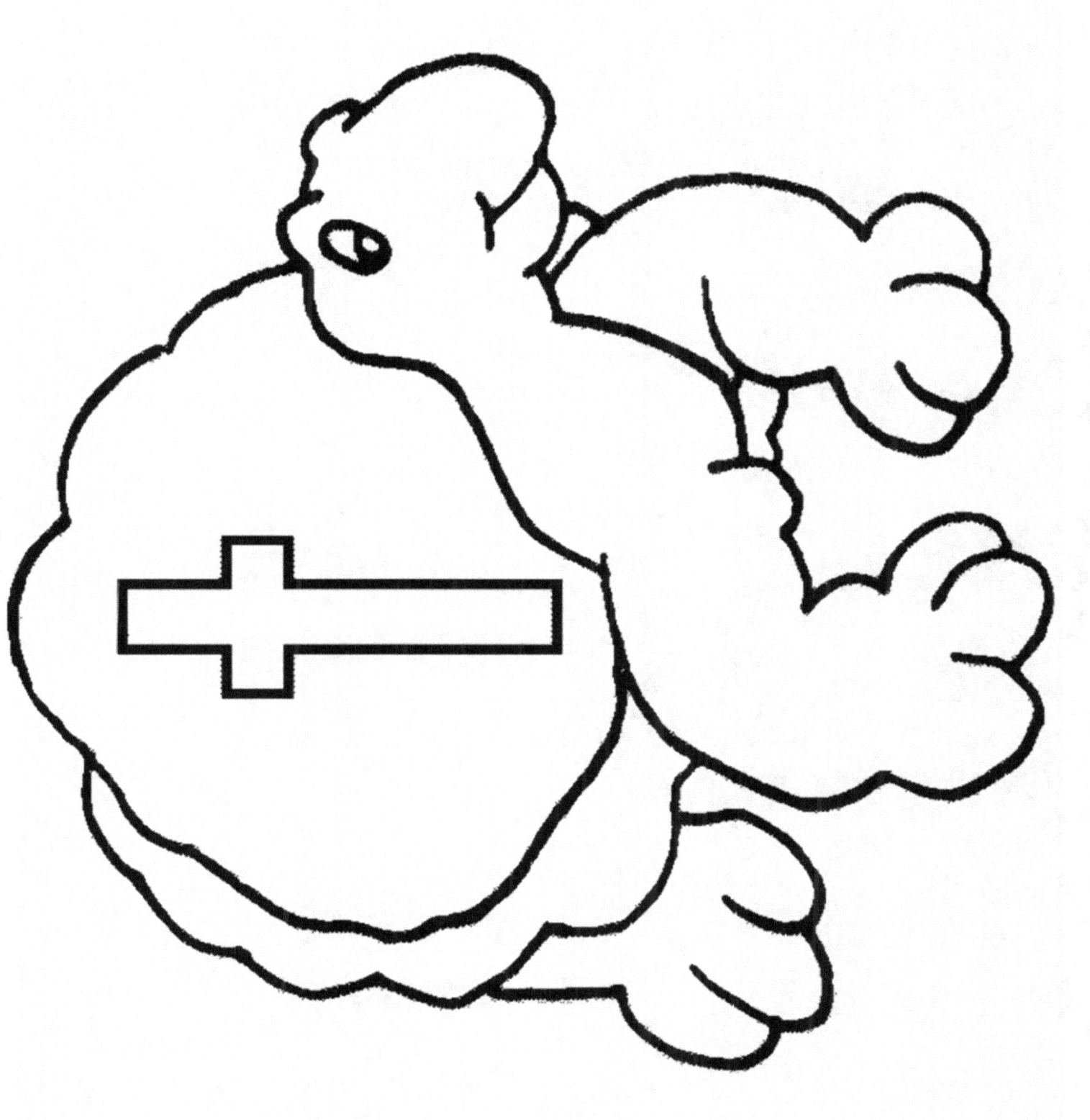

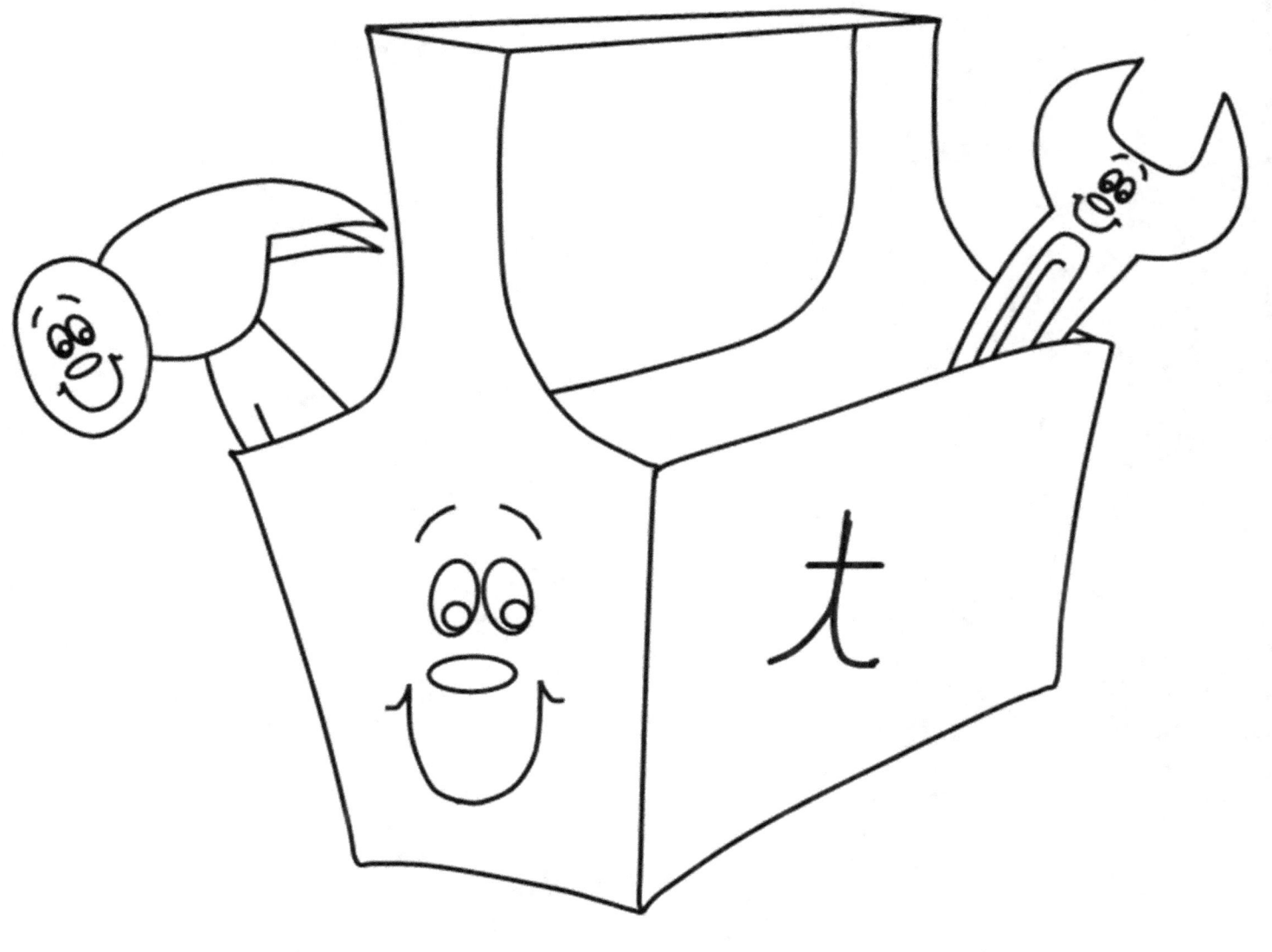

Trace the steps for making the letter t on the following line.

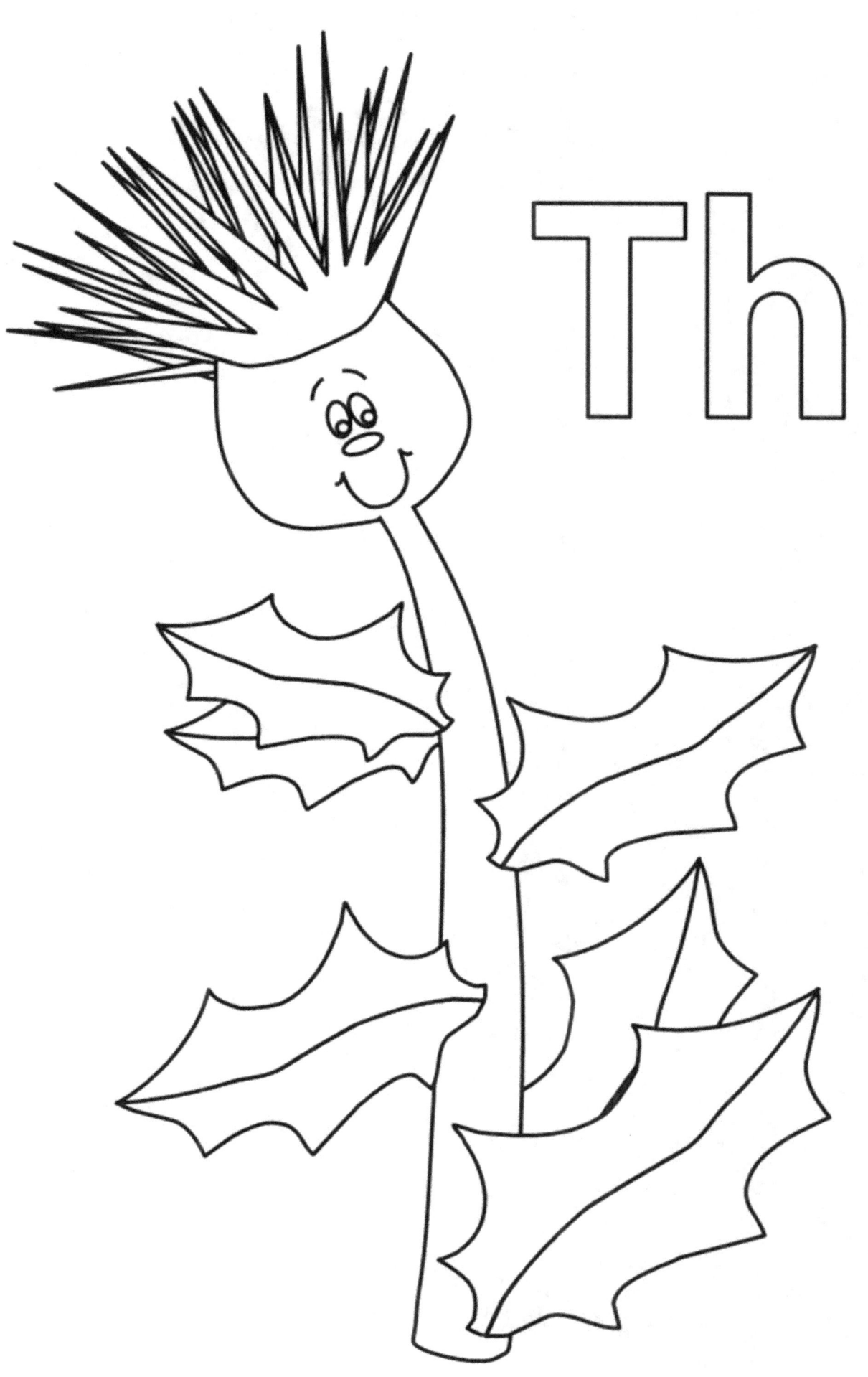

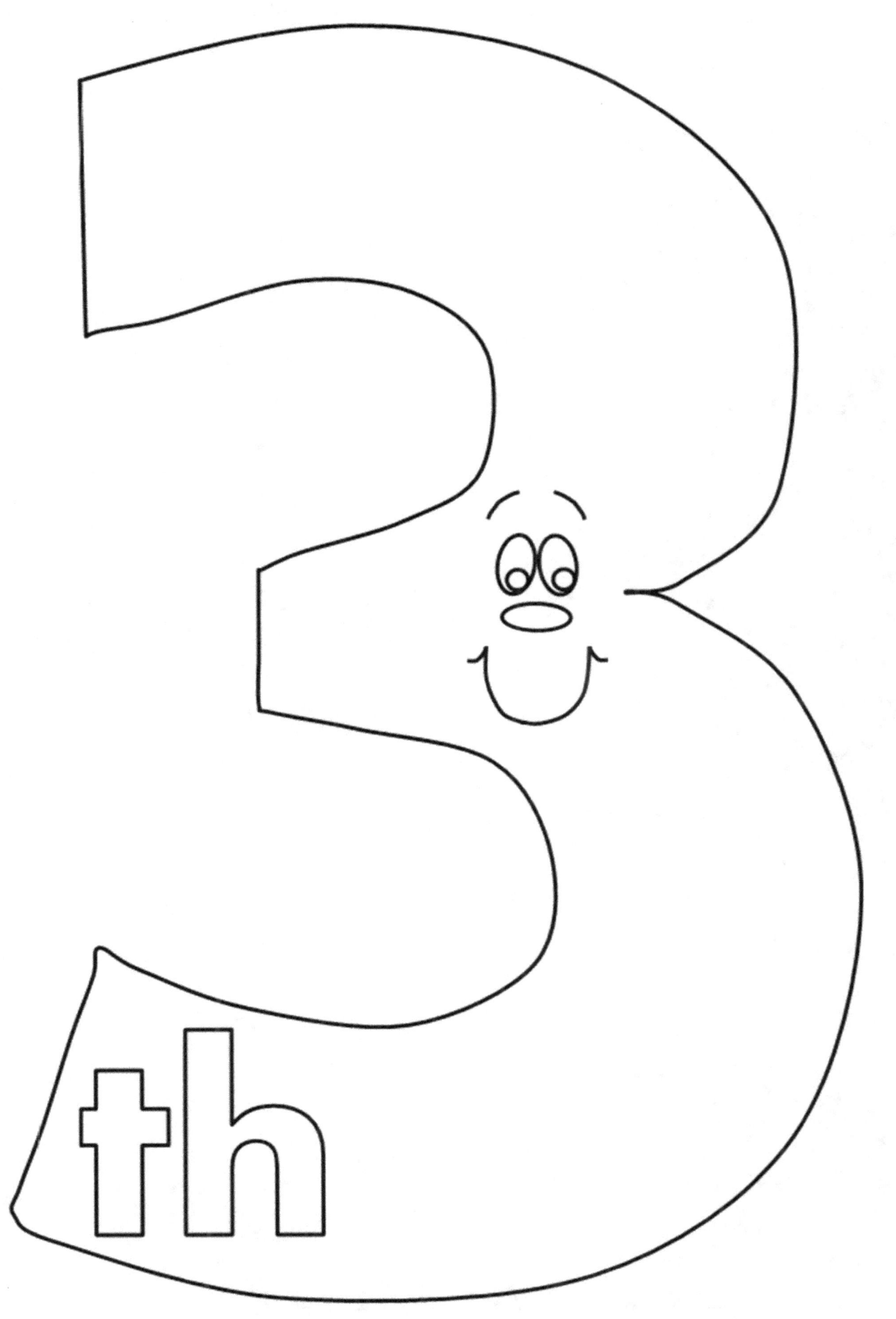

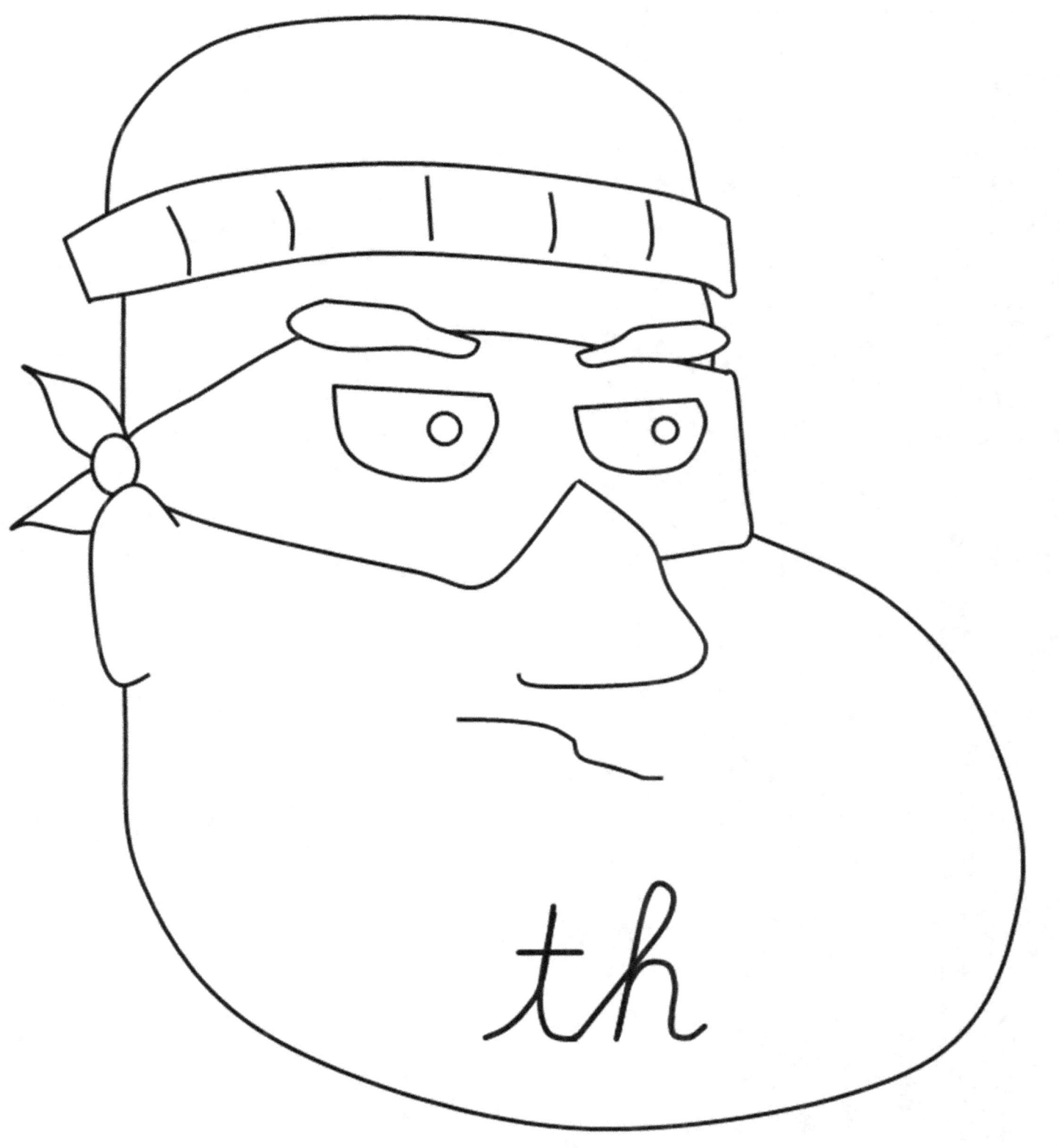

Trace the steps for making the letter th on the following line.

_t_ _th_ _th_ _th_ _th_ _th_

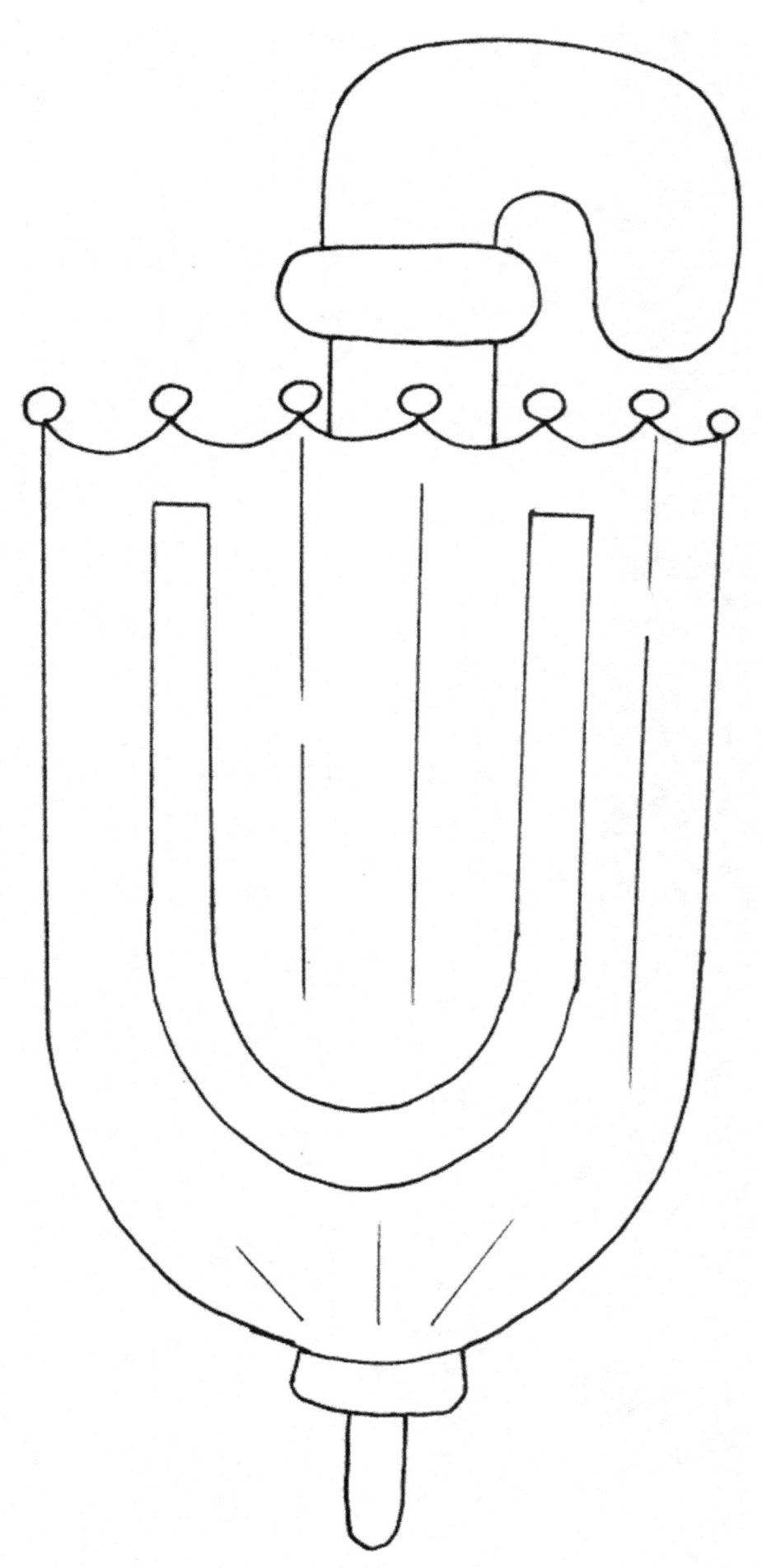

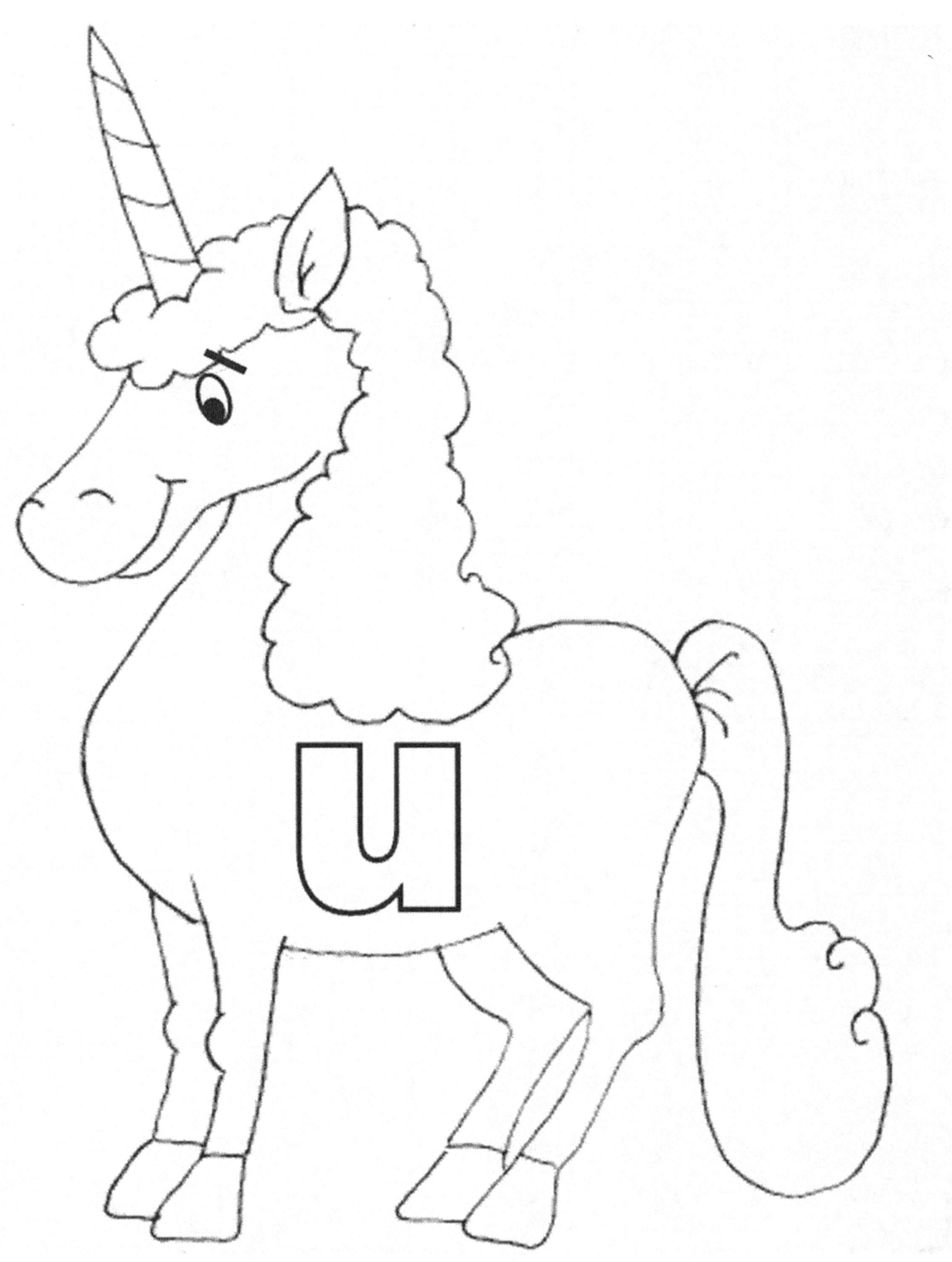

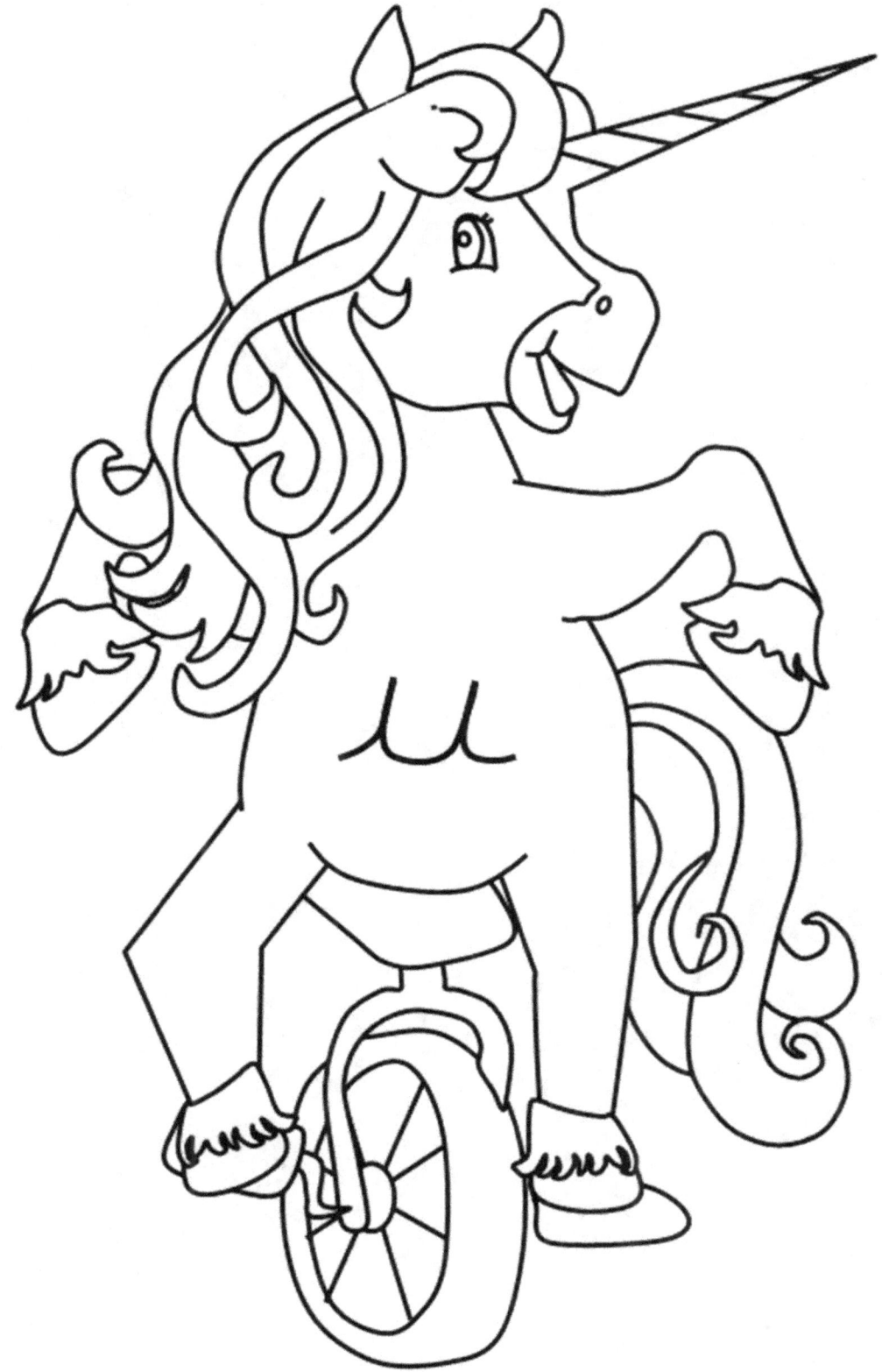

Trace the steps for making the letter u on the following line.

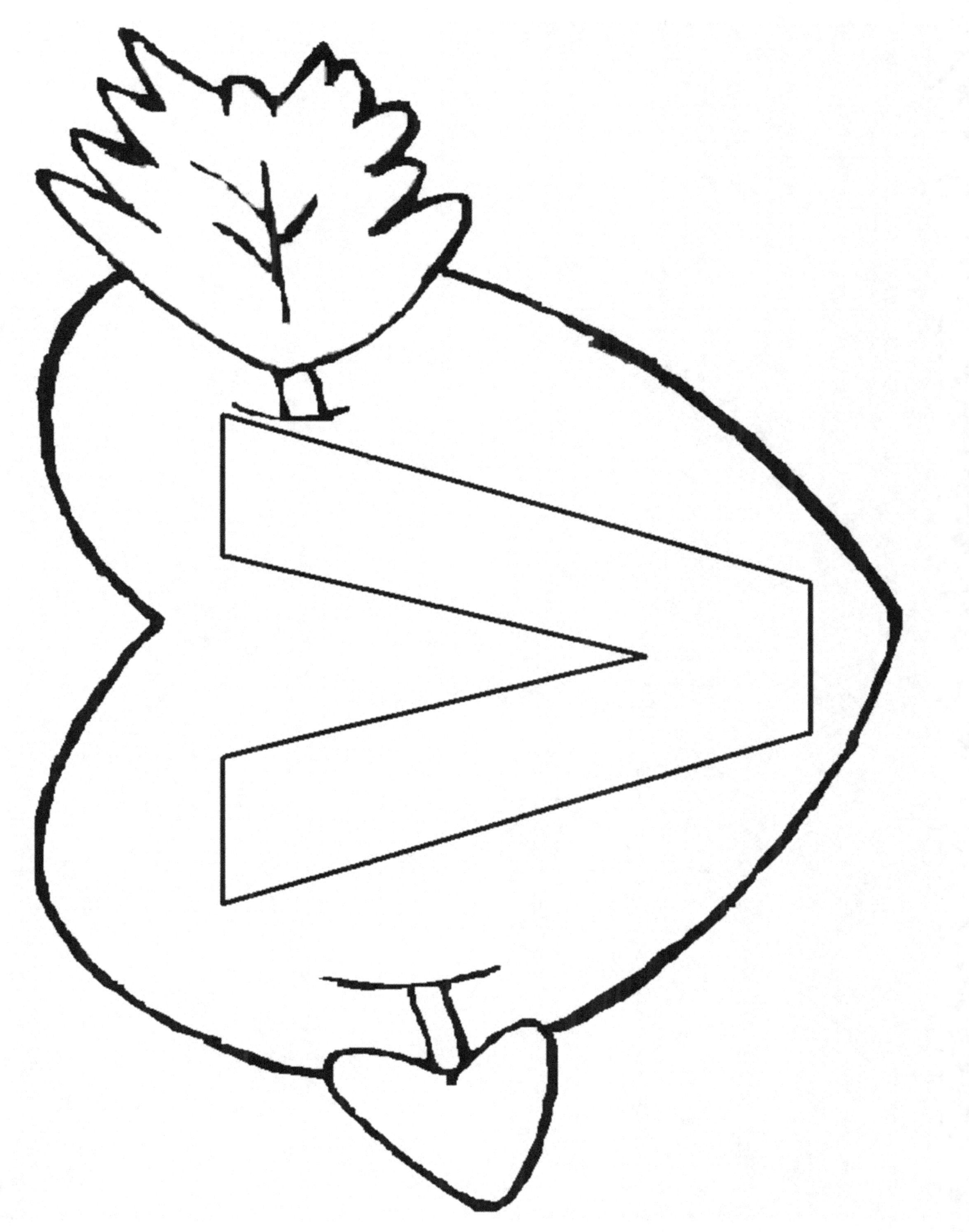

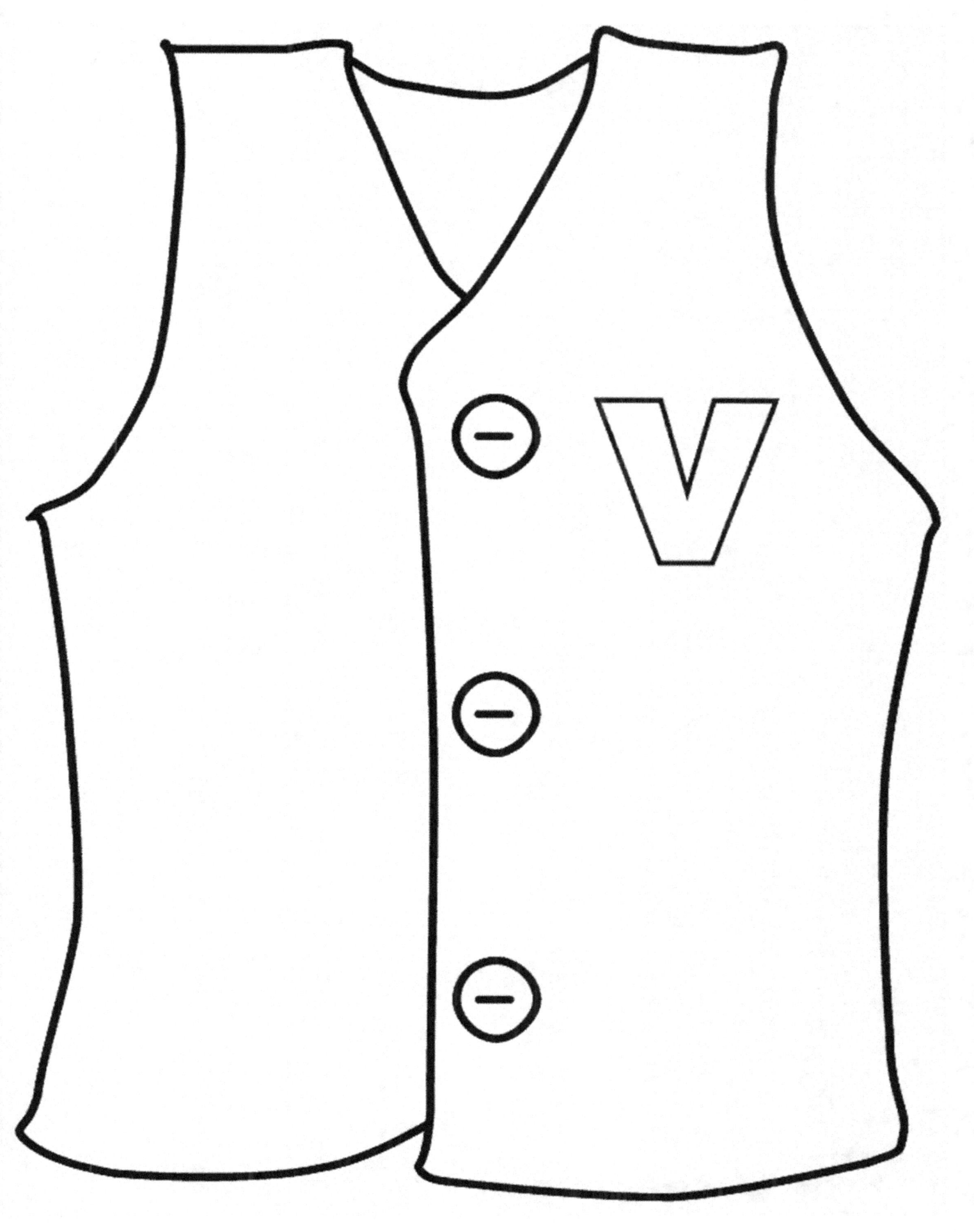

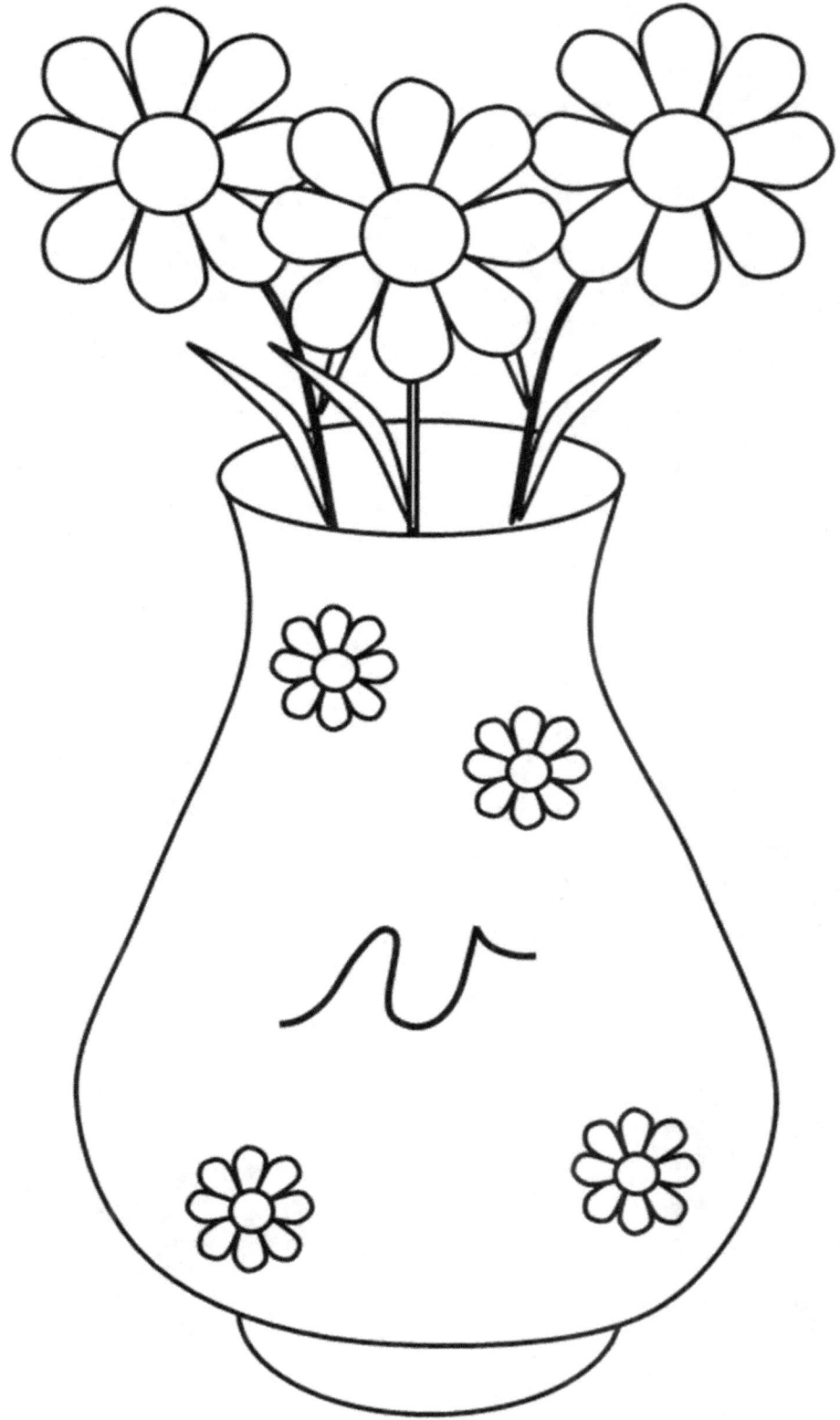

Trace the steps for making the letter v on the following line.

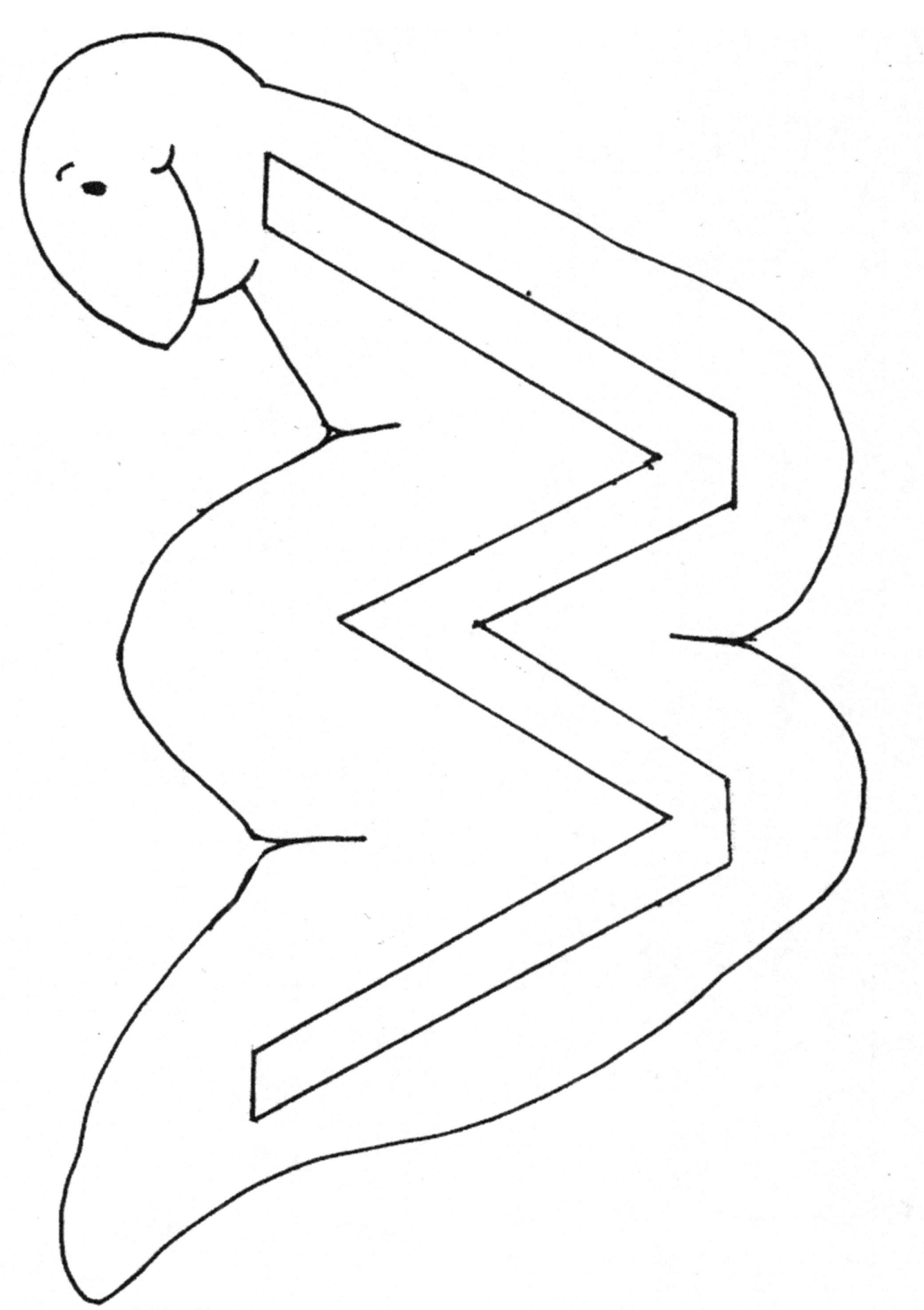

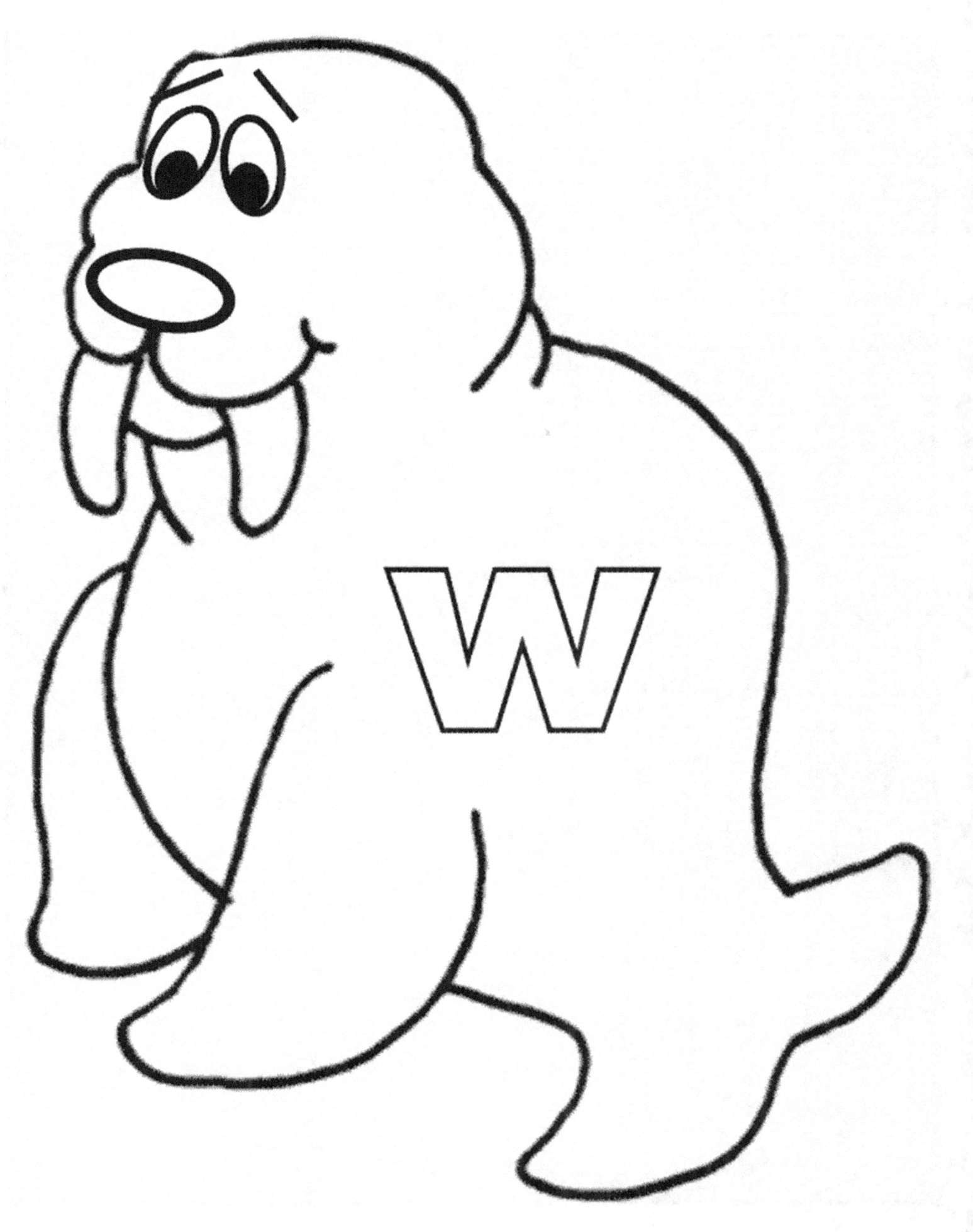

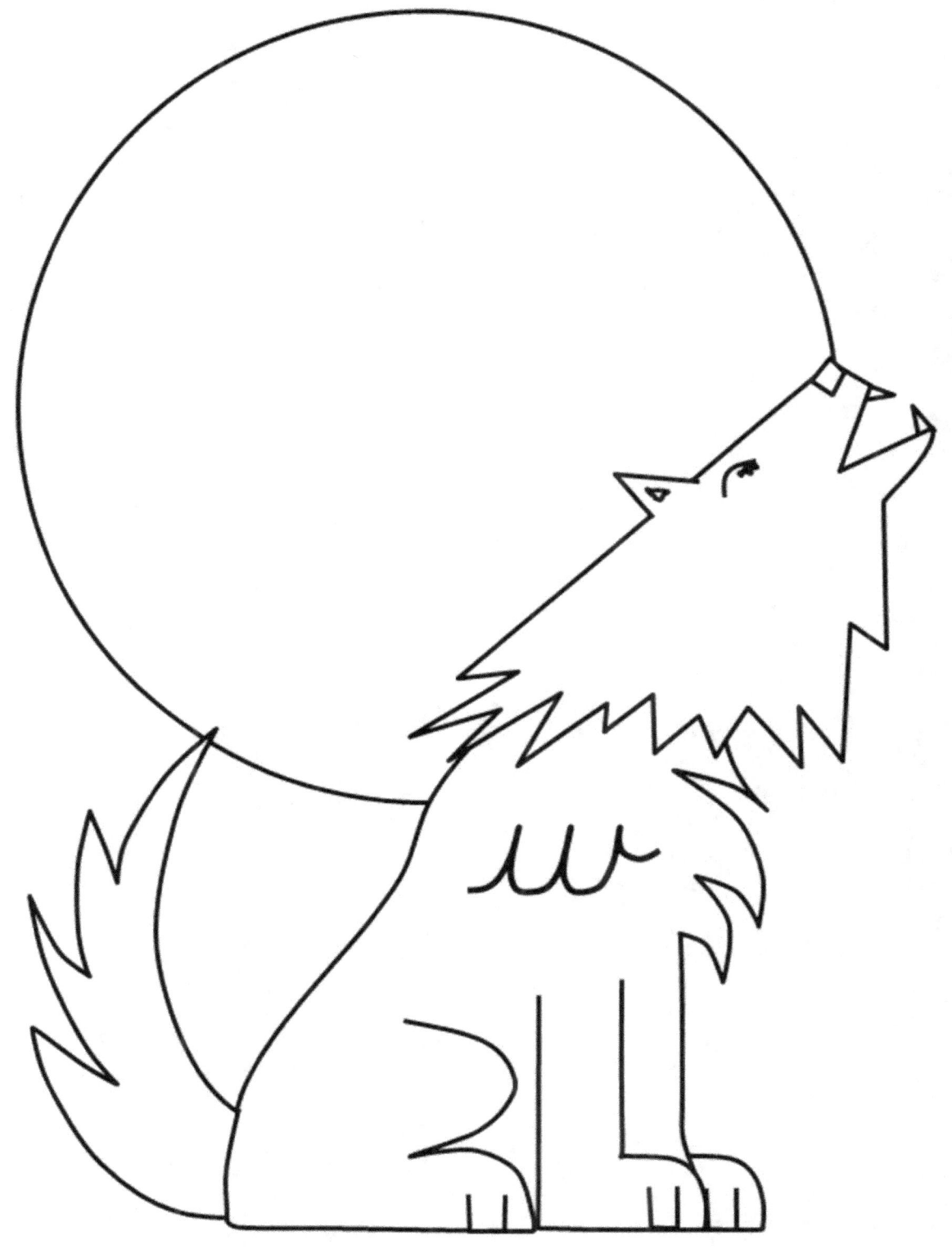

Trace the steps for making the letter w on the following line.

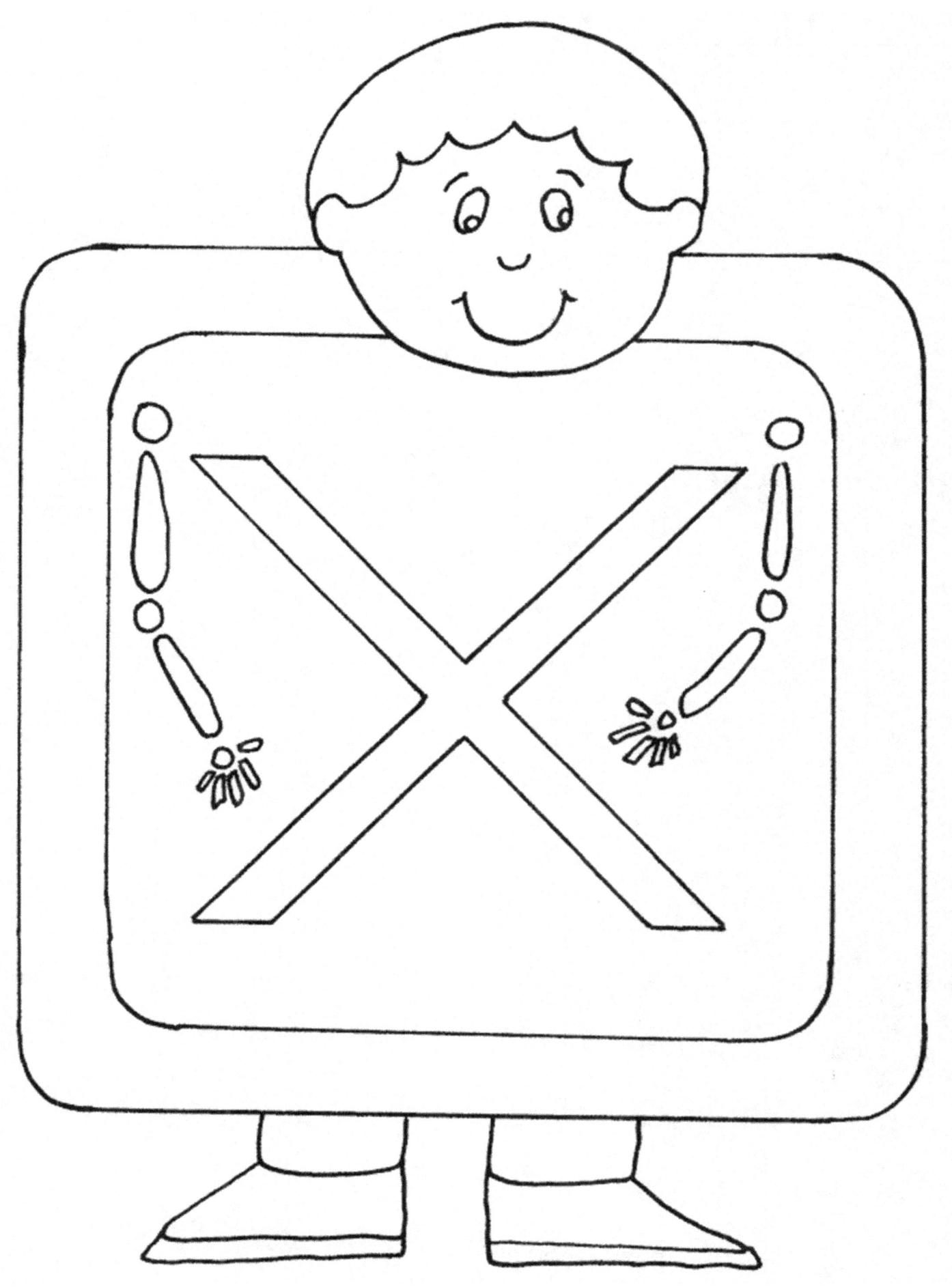

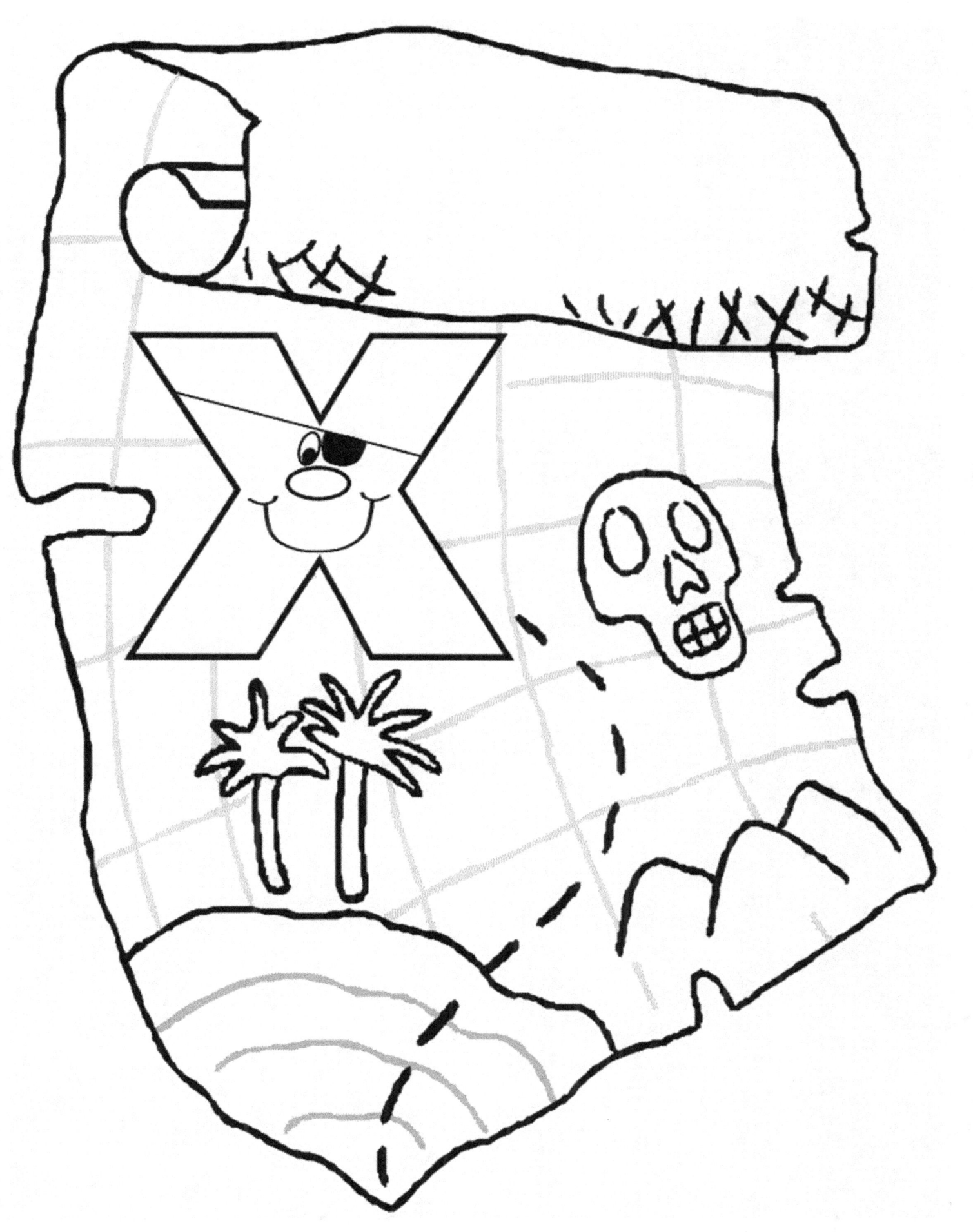

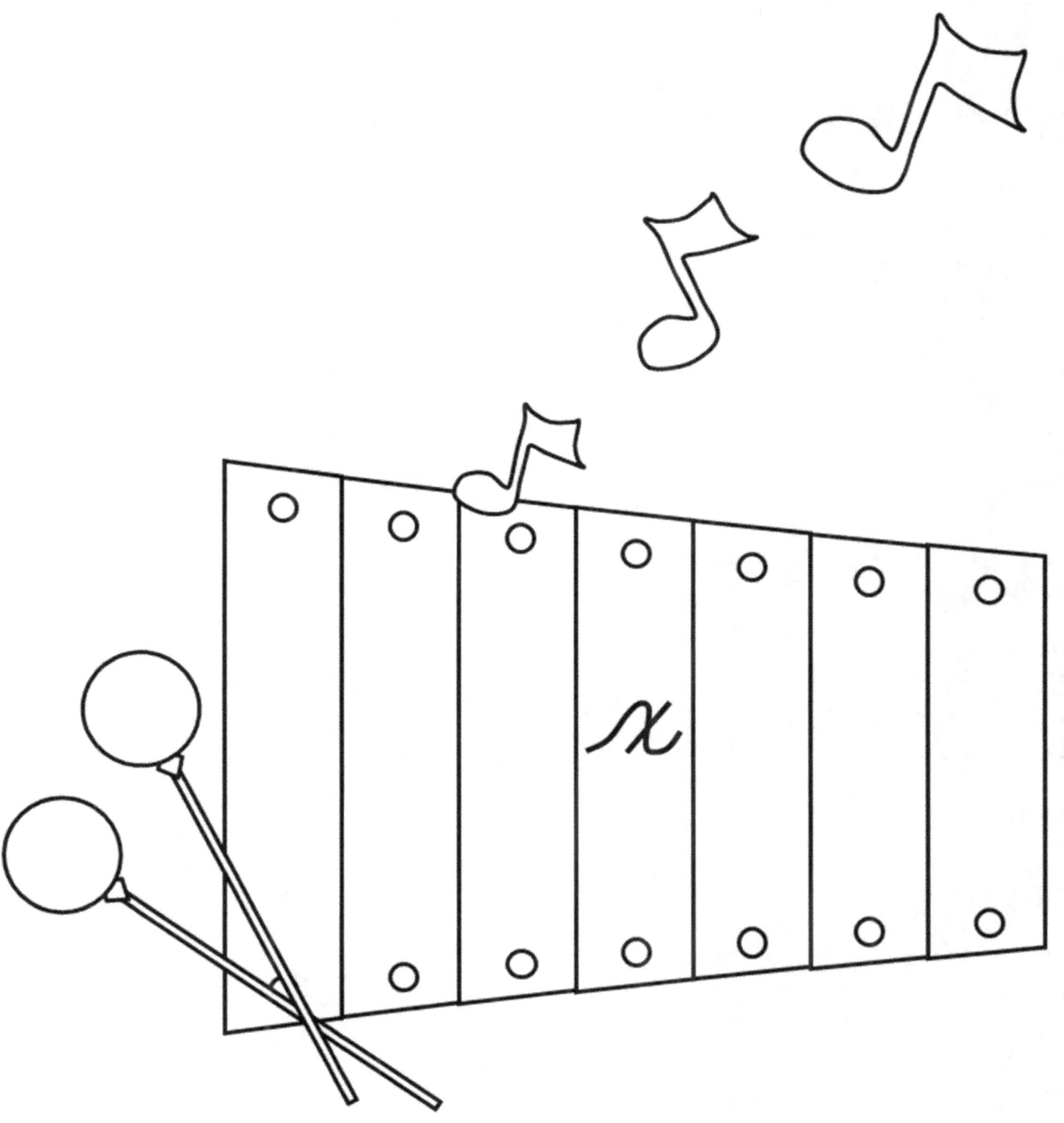

Trace the steps for making the letter x on the following line.

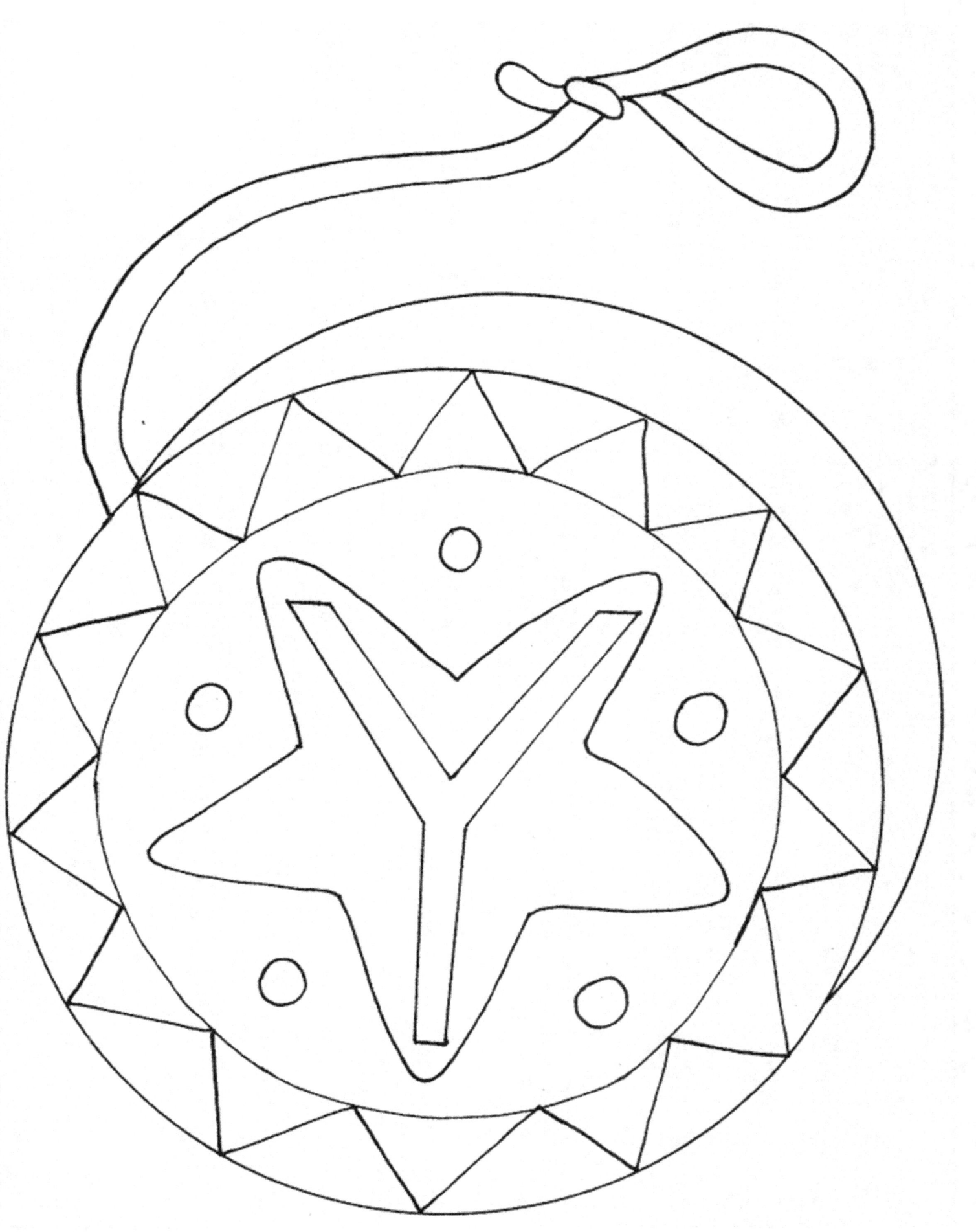

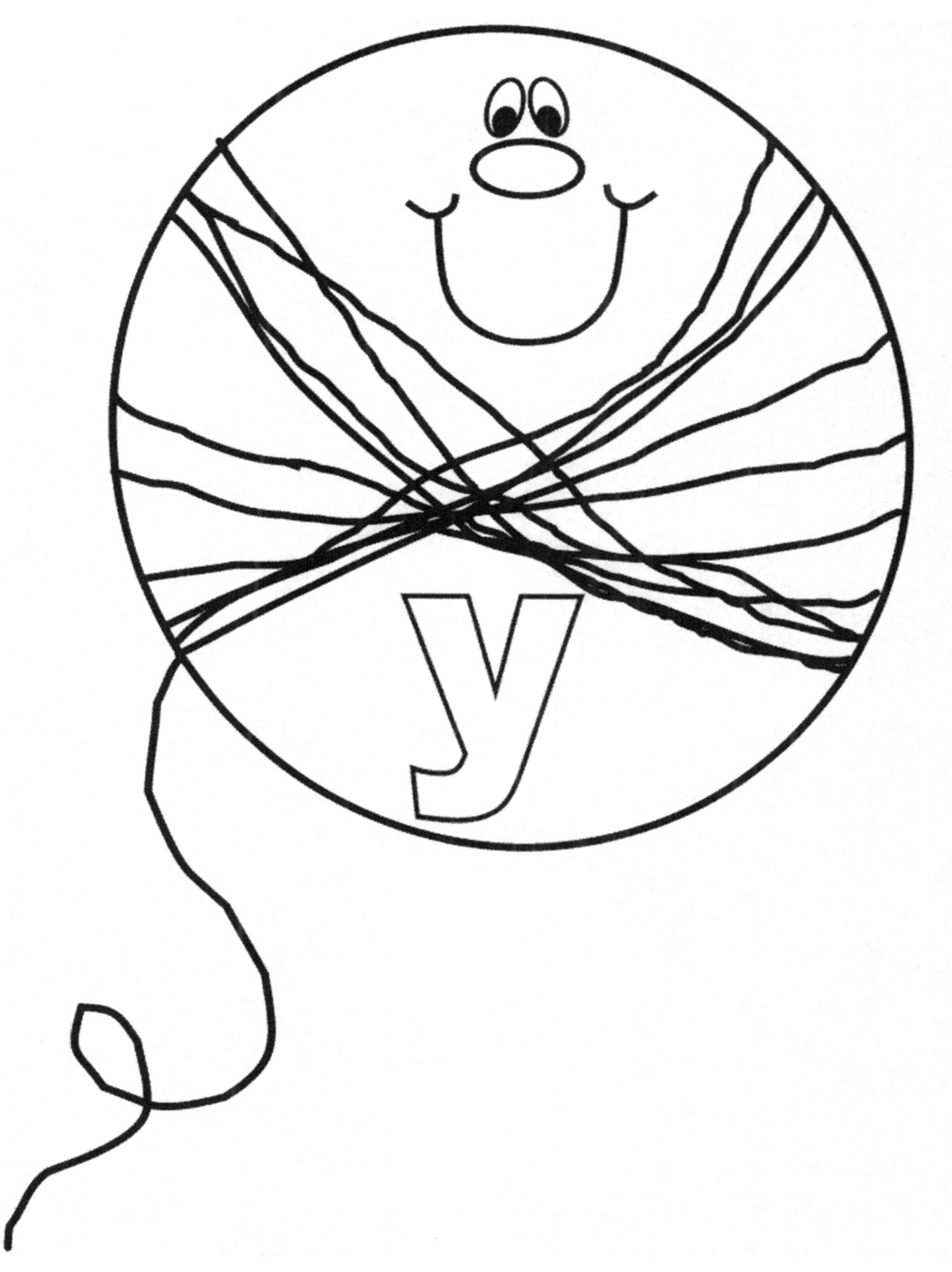

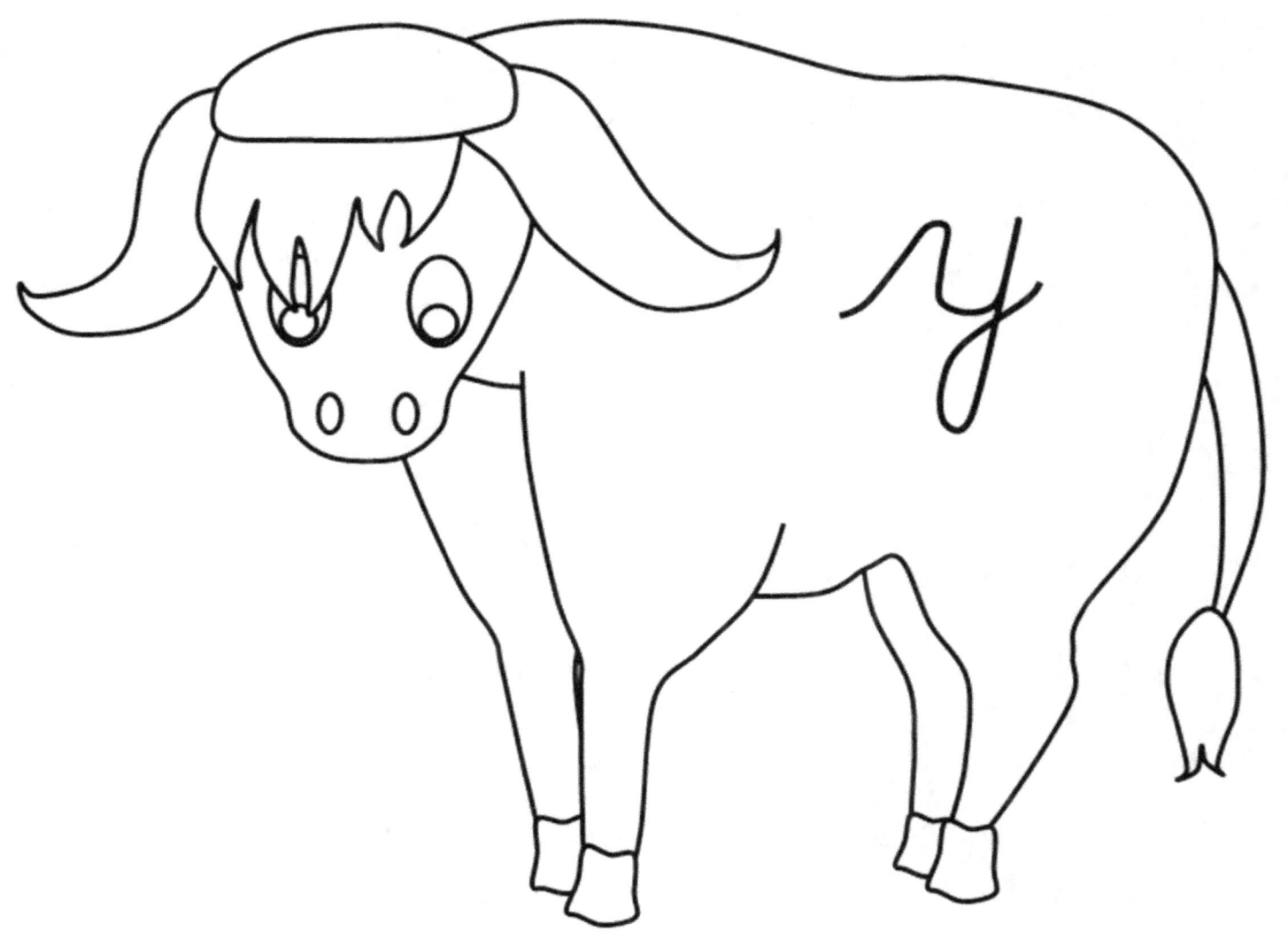

Trace the steps for making the letter y on the following line.

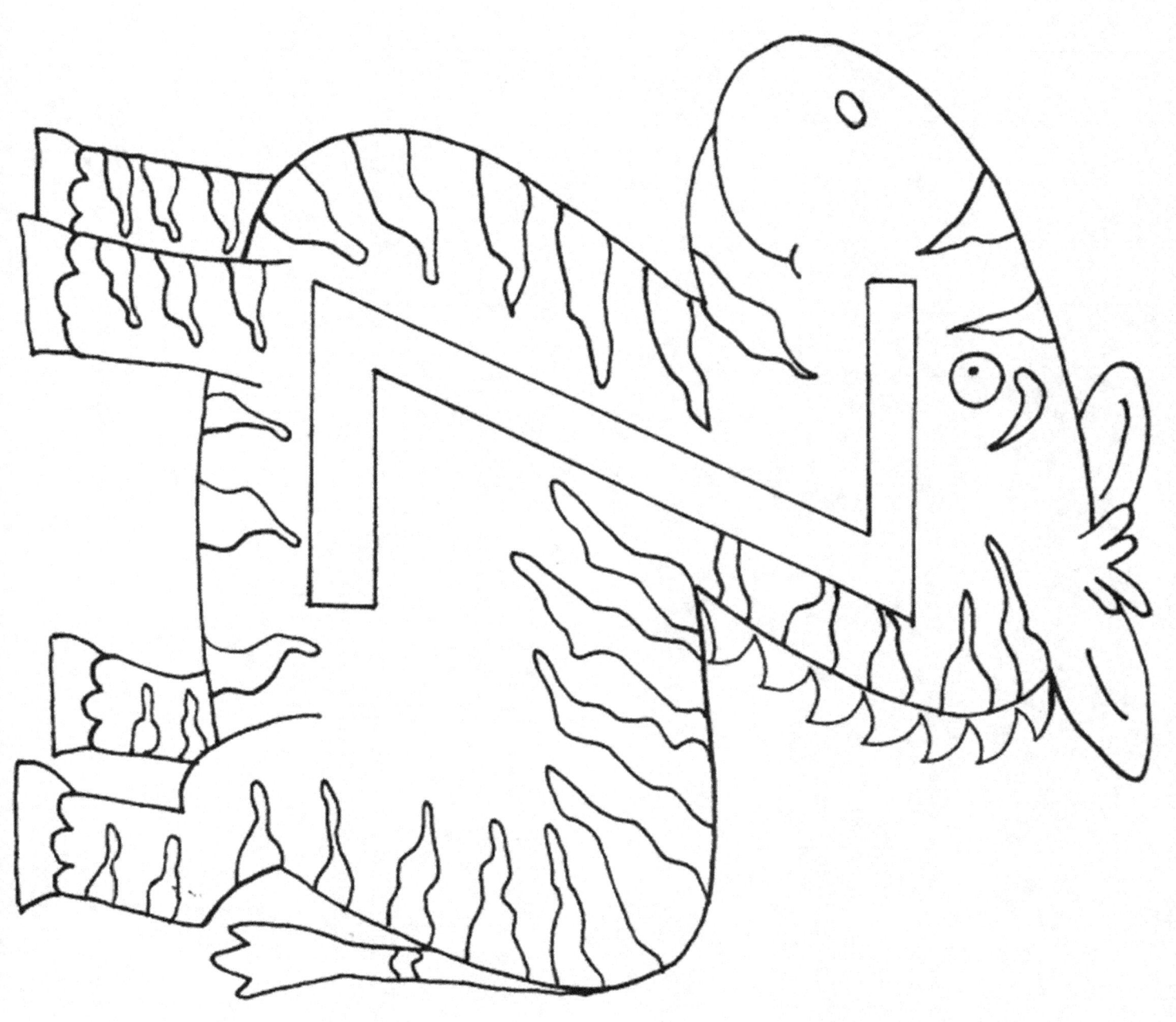

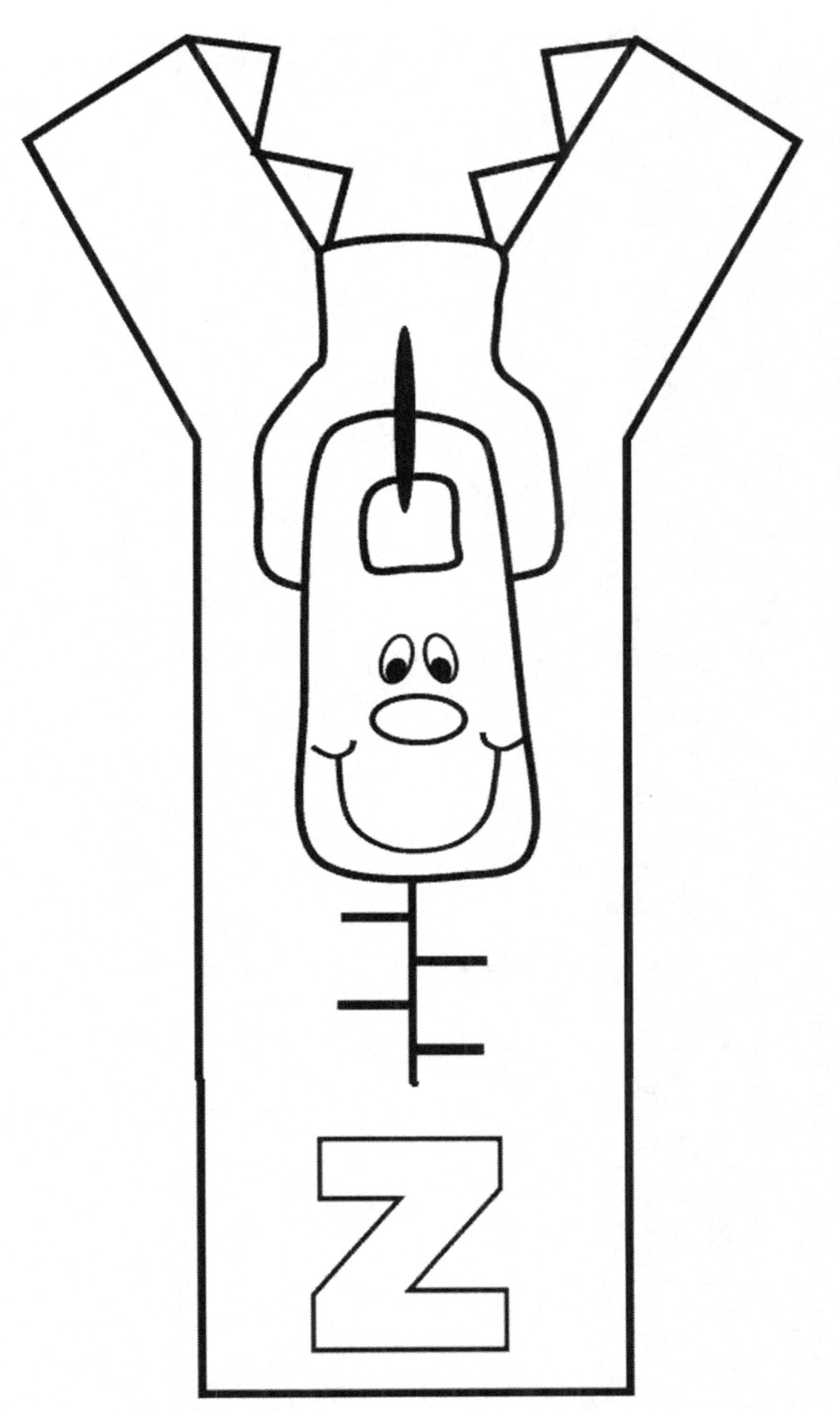

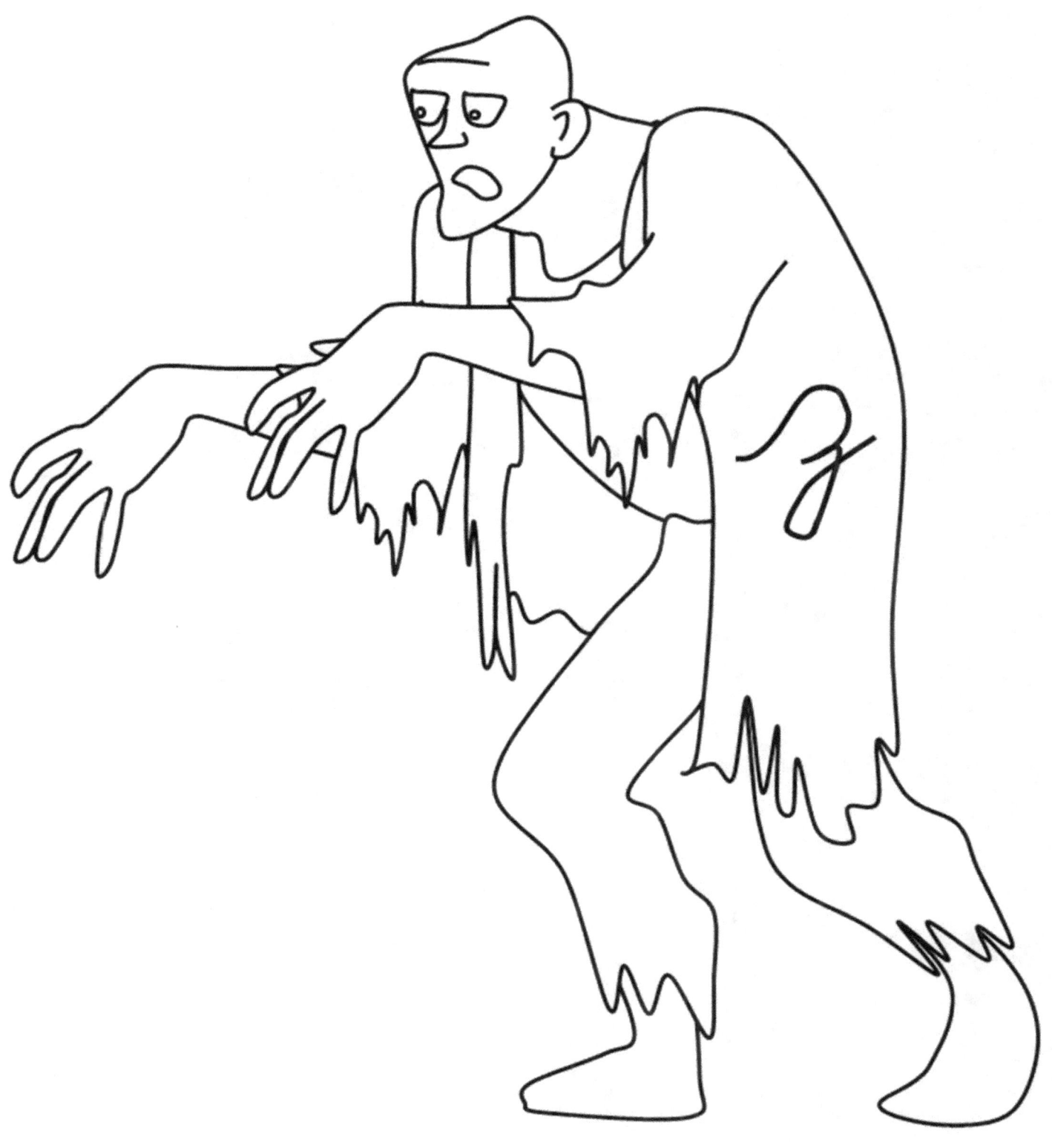

Trace the steps for making the letter z on the following line.